# EV ENGINEERING FUNDAMENTALS

## A BEGINNER'S GUIDE TO E-MOBILITY

ASHHAR AHMED SHAIKH

**Thanks to the Almighty!!!**

**This book is dedicated to my parents, family, professors, and mentors.**

# Contents

*Foreword* *vii*
*Preface* *ix*
*Acknowledgements* *xi*
*Prologue* *xiii*
1. Transportation System 1
2. History Of The Automobile 3
3. Challenges In Transportation System 6
4. E-mobility 9
5. E-mobility Evolution 11
6. Ev Market 14
7. Ev Ecosystem 17
8. E-mobility In India 19
9. India's Electric Vehicle Journey 21
10. Gasoline Vehicle 24
11. Hybrid Electric Vehicle 27
12. Plug-in Hybrid Electric Vehicle 31
13. Battery Electric Vehicle 35
14. Hydrogen Fuel Cell Electric Vehicle 38
15. Motors For Electric Vehicle 41
16. Batteries For Electric Vehicles 51
17. Controllers For Electric Vehicles 61
18. Converters For Electric Vehicles 64
19. Chargers For Electric Vehicles 67
20. Design Of Powertrain For Electric Vehicle 75
21. Ev Safety & Maintenance 80
22. Future Mobility 90
Bibliography 97
Coefficients 99

# Contents

Infographic 101

# FOREWORD

Electric vehicles are innovative and upcoming technology in the mobility and power sector that have many economic and environmental benefits. The electric vehicle outlook is swiftly changing as both technology and interest evolve, and the coming years will see more & more EVs on the roads. The book "EV Engineering Fundamentals" by Engineer Ashhar Ahmed provides valuable insights into various elements of the EV Ecosystem. Book has very well covered EV Technology, Challenges, and Opportunities. This book is a valuable addition to existing knowledge and is especially intended for students, faculties, researchers, and EV Enthusiasts. - Spencer Tweneboa Korankye (Founder EV4Africa).

# PREFACE

Today, the Electric vehicle is seen as a possible replacement for traditional automobiles, to address the issue of rising pollution, global warming, depleting natural resources, etc. EVs have drawn a considerable amount of interest in the past decade amid a rising carbon footprint and other environmental impacts of fuel-based vehicles. Many existing automobile manufacturers and new startups/ companies have put a significant effort into transforming the conventional vehicle into an Electric Vehicle that provides a green and reliable solution. This book is the result of experience: From one side the experience of teaching courses such as EV Architecture, EV Design, EV Powertrain, EV Safety, and more to students of Engineering; on another side the experience of heading product development in an EV startup offering EV Conversion Kits & Services. This book is addressed primarily to students of engineering and secondarily to all technicians and designers working in this field. It is also addressed to all enthusiasts who are looking for technical guidance in EV Design & Development.

# Acknowledgements

The author would like to put on record his thanks to all the stakeholders of the EV Ecosystem that have made this book possible. In addition, I would like to thank friends and colleagues who have provided valuable comments and advice. I am also indebted to my family who has helped me while I devoted time and energy to this project. Special thanks to Spencer Tweneboa Korankye, for reading and commenting on the draft copy of the Book.

# PROLOGUE

The global automotive future looks electric. Concerted policy push and innovations from automotive manufacturers are fast making e-mobility viable. While we are heading towards E-Mobility Mission, we need to work on creating EV Ecosystem. Fostering Skills, Innovations, Employability, and Entrepreneurship will contribute a significant part to EV Ecosystem Development. In the coming time, there will be a huge demand for Skilled-Workforce in EV Industry. So, knowing the functionality of an EV is very essential for an engineering student irrespective of his or her stream. This book is a beginner's guide to future mobility.

## About the author

Ashhar Ahmed Shaikh is an EV Enthusiast & Entrepreneur with a demonstrated history of working in the EV & Edu-tech Industry. Till now, He has visited 100+ Engineering Institutions in India & abroad as Keynote Speaker and trained thousands of students & faculties through AICTE FDP/ TEQIP / Skill Development Programs. He is contributing to EV Ecosystem development by fostering Skills & Innovation in the field of future mobility.

## Contact author


- Email: ashhar@skillshark.in
- LinkedIn: www.linkedin.com/in/ashharahmed/

# I

# Transportation System

Transportation plays an important role in the growth of a country's economy; in shaping overall productivity, quality of life, and access to goods and services. An effective and well-devised transportation system plays a notable role in the economic development of a country. Good physical connections between urban and rural areas are very important for economic growth. Since the early 1990s, India's growing economy has witnessed an increase in demand for transportation infrastructure and services. However, the industry has been unable to keep up with growing demand. Therefore, significant improvements in this sector are needed to support the country's continued economic growth and reduce poverty.

- **Roadways:** In today's time, roads are the dominant mode of transportation in India. They carry almost 85 percent of the country's passenger transport and more than 60 percent of its cargo. The density of the Indian highway network is 0.66 km per square kilometer of land. Rural Roads are a Lifeline for Villages in India, Connecting Hinterland to Social Services and markets.

- **Railways:** Indian Railways is one of the largest railways under a single management authority. It is one of the world's huge employers. The railways play a principal role in carrying passengers and cargo across India.

- **Waterways:** India has major, minor and intermediate ports along its more than 7500 km long coastline. Ports play a very important role in improving foreign trade in a growing economy. These ports help expand domestic trade in petroleum products, iron ore, and coal. The future potential for the port sector is very huge.

- **Airways:** India has 120+ airports, including 15+ international airports. The dramatic increase in both passenger and freight air traffic in recent years has placed a heavy burden on major airports in the country. Passenger traffic is predicted to grow. And it is estimated that the aviation industry, currently the 7$^{th}$ largest in the World (As per 2022 ranking data), will acquire investments to keep pace with the increasing needs.

# II

# History of the automobile

### *1) Invention of the Wheel:*

The wheel is considered one of the most important mechanical inventions to date. The wheel has been used by man since the beginning of civilization. Most primary technologies since the invention of the wheel have been based on its fundamentals. The invention of the wheel possibly happened in the late Neolithic age. It is likely that along with other technological developments, it gave rise to the early Bronze Age.

4500 BC: Invention of the potter's the wheel, Chalcolithic.

4500–3300 BC: Chalcolithic, earliest wheeled vehicles, domestication of the horse.

3300–2200 BC: Early Bronze Age.

2200–1550 BC: Middle Bronze Age, the invention of the spoked wheel and the chariot.

Since the Industrial Revolution, the wheel has been a key element of nearly every machine constructed by mankind.

### *2) Wheel cart:*

Wheel cart is designed for transport, using two wheels. A handcart is manually pulled or pushed by one or more people. However, history tells us that animals, instead of men, were used for pulling the vehicles, as they were more powerful. Normally, a cart or vehicle was pulled by a pair of draught animals.

## *3) Invention of the automobile:*

Engineers gradually improved the carriage design. At the same time, work was being done on a self-propelled system. A system that can operate without the power of humans or animals. The very first such model was developed in the form of a toy in the year 1672. This was a steam engine, in which the power of steam was used to provide impulse or momentum to the toy. Further iterations continued in various parts of the world. The first car powered by an internal combustion engine appeared in the year 1806. The fuel used for this was "fuel gas" rather than "steam". The process of using fuel was different. The steam engine requires ‘external combustion' whereas fuel gas uses the principle of the internal combustion. Meanwhile, engineers continued to revise designs till the year 1885 when the first modern gasoline-or petrol-fueled engine was made in Europe. The first practical model in the year 1885 was designed and patented by Karl Benz, a German engineer. During World War I and II, the automobile industry paid a lot of attention to developing defense vehicles. This resulted in the development of several new vehicles, like battle tanks and jeeps. However, there were some very interesting designs in the passenger area as well during this time.

## *4) Automobile post World War II:*

Post World War II, the automotive industry automotive showed rapid modernization in the 1950s and 1960s. Edsel, Chevrolet, and many new car models were introduced. In the U.S., the road network was built after World War II. This road network was quite modern with long highways stretching across the country. Notably, the U.S. has a large mainland and wide geography, which allows open and wide roads to be built. Models like the Beetle appear very tiny on these roads. The big three in the automotive industry, General Motors, Ford, and Chrysler, have embarked on the development of large, fast-moving cars for the American streets. In the 1950s and 1960s, Edsel, Buick, Pontiac Firebird, Chevrolet Impala, etc., were some of the big cars that came on American highways. However, things changed after the year 1973. This year was the first year of the "oil crisis". Petrol has begun to become more expensive. Now, suddenly, Americans were looking for a more economical design.

Meanwhile, Japan has quietly but determinedly developed cars for the global market. Several Japanese companies emerged, including Toyota, Mazda, Mitsubishi, and Suzuki. As a result, when the oil crisis occurred, these companies were very well-positioned to roll out smaller, compact, economic models in the U.S. Since then, companies like Toyota, and Honda have been steadily increasing their market presence worldwide. There are few design & technical aspects that differentiate modern vehicles from antiques. The modern era has been focusing on standardization, platform sharing, and computer-aided design.

## *5) Automotive Industry in India:*

The automotive industry in India started with the import of cars for royal families, which perhaps started in the 1920s. India did not have any manufacturing capability of its own for many years. Hindustan Motors is one of the first automobile manufacturers in India, founded in 1942 by B.M. Birla. It was a leader in car sales until the 1980s. Hindustan Motors was the producer of the Ambassador car, widely used as a taxicab and a government limousine. As we can see, the Indian automobile industry began importing cars in the 1920s and manufacturing in the 1940s. With continued progress, many Indian companies like Maruti, Tata, and Mahindra have become big global names. They have expertise in design and manufacturing with their research and development. The automotive industry in India is one of the largest in the world and one of the fastest-growing globally.

# III

# Challenges in Transportation System

The automotive industry, which contributes to roughly 3 % of global GDP, is a major industrial and economic force worldwide. The development of internal combustion engine vehicles, especially automobiles, is one of the greatest achievements of modern technology. Automobiles have made great contributions to the growth of contemporary society by satisfying many of its needs for convenient mobility in everyday life. The rapid development of the automotive industry, unlike that of any other industry, has prompted the progress of human society from a primitive one to a highly developed industrial society. The automotive industry and the other industries that serve it constitute the backbone of the world's economy and employ the greatest share of the working population. However, the large number of automobiles in use around the world has caused and continues to cause serious problems for the environment and human life. Air pollution, global warming, and the rapid depletion of the Earth's petroleum resources are now problems of paramount concern.

| Fuel Type | Best for Vehicles | Average Price Per Litre in Delhi (June-2022) |
|---|---|---|
| Gasoline | 4 wheeler cars, bikes | ₹101.84 |
| Diesel | Trucks, trains, public buses | ₹ 89.87 |
| CNG | Passenger cars, buses, vans, trucks | ₹75.61 |
| Bio-Diesel | Diesel-powered vehicles, and specially manufactured vans, trucks and SUVs | ₹69.44 |
| Liquid Petroleum Gas | Light-duty bio-fuel vehicles | ₹60.08 |
| Ethanol or Methanol | Used in racing cars. It is blended with gasoline for use in existing on-road vehicles | ₹46.66 (C-heavy molasses) ₹59.08 (B-heavy molasses) |

Table 1 - Fuel Types

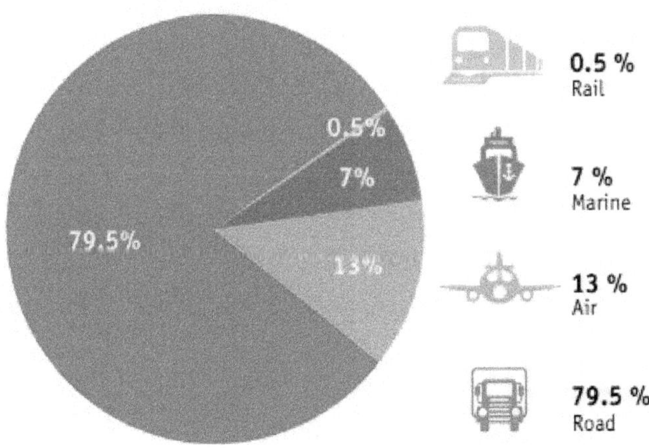


Figure 1- Emissions

The key challenges the automotive industry is facing are

- Depletion of Fossil Fuels.
- Increasing Cost of Petrol/Diesel.
- Pollution.
- Green House Gases.
- Climate Change.
- Environmental Impact.
- High Cost of Operation.
- Strict Emission Norms.

Automotive Industry is exploring solutions to combat the above challenges. The present optimum solution seems to be the adoption of Electric Vehicles. But the real impact of EVs in terms of operational economics and pollution control can be examined only after a few years of adoption. Also to extract significant output from E-Mobility, we need to power EVs with renewable energy resources to eliminate indirect pollution via Coal-based Power generation. Like any other industry, automotive and allied sectors are going through fast-paced technological innovations. Increasing funding for R&D of connected vehicles and autonomous vehicles, the launch of semi-autonomous vehicles in recent years, and the growing integration of IoT in automobiles validate the aforesaid fact.

# IV
# E-Mobility

Considering the climate change commitments made by the Government of India during the COP21 Summit held in Paris to reduce emission intensity by 33-35% by 2030 from 2005 levels, it is appropriate to introduce alternative means in the transport sector which can be coupled with India's rapid economic growth, rising urbanization, travel demand and country's energy security. Electric mobility presents a viable alternative in addressing these challenges when packaged with innovative pricing solutions, appropriate technology, and support infrastructure. Electric mobility will also contribute to balancing energy demand, energy storage, and environmental sustainability. Electric vehicles powered by renewable energy resources are the best combination for pollution reduction. Electric mobility comes with zero or very low tailpipe emissions and much lower noise. It can provide a major boost to the economic and industrial competitiveness, attracting investments. The government of India has undertaken multiple initiatives to promote the manufacturing and adoption of electric vehicles in India. With the support of the government, electric vehicles have started penetrating the Indian market.

## *Electric Vehicle & Benefits*

In recent years, the demand for electric vehicles has increased throughout India. The Covid-19 pandemic is accelerating the acceptance of personal mobility. And the constant rise in gasoline and diesel prices is fueling the demand for electric vehicles. Compared to traditional ICE models, electric vehicles have proven to be more efficient as well as free of emissions.

Overall, EVs are cost-effective because they have the best operational economics. Another advantage of electric vehicles is tax incentives. There are several benefits to be gained from an electric vehicle. The main benefits are:

1. **Economical:**

    - EVs have fewer moving parts as compared to ICE, thus EVs need less maintenance.
    - Higher efficiency, lower fuel cost and lower operational cost makes EVs more economical than ICE vehicles.

2. **Improved Air quality:**

    - EVs have no tailpipe emission as compared to ICE vehicles. Adopting EVs will help in reducing local air pollution.
    - Shifting to EVs will reduce Greenhouse Gas (GHG) emissions that get emitted from running an ICE vehicle.

3. **Convenience:**

    - EVs have no gears and are much easier to drive than ICE vehicles.
    - The lack of combustion and mechanical drivetrain makes EVs much quieter.
    - Comfortably charge at home.
    - Upfront incentives from Government to EV owners.
    - The incentive for scrapping ICE vehicles.
    - EV owners can claim income tax deductions up to Rs 150,000 under Section 80EEB.
    - Reduced dependence on imported fossil fuels for the Country.

# V

# E-Mobility Evolution

Electrification is one of the best ways to establish clean and energy-efficient transportation. Electric vehicles have been in use for much longer than today's Tesla Motors and the General Motors EV1 in the late 1990s. Electric cars appeared long before the type of internal combustion engine. And dreamers never stopped trying to run electric cars on the road or as a business proposal.

- First Small Scale Electric Cars (1828-1830): Small scale electric cars by Innovators in Hungary, the Netherlands, and the US.
- First Crude Electric Vehicle Developed (1832): Around 1832, Robert Anderson develops the first crude electric vehicle.
- First Electric Vehicle Debuts in the U.S. (1889 -1891): William Morrison, from Des Moines, Iowa, creates the first successful electric vehicle in the U.S. His car is little more than an electrified wagon.
- The popularity of Electric Cars (1899): Electric Cars Gain Popularity Compared to the gas and steam-powered automobiles at the time, electric cars are quiet, easy to drive, and didn't emit smelly pollutants -- quickly becoming popular with urban residents, especially women.
- Electric Cars Reach Their Peak (1900): By the turn of the century, electric vehicles are all the rage in the U.S., accounting for around a third of all vehicles on the road.
- Electric Vehicle Batteries (1901): Many innovators took note of the electric car's high demand and explored ways to improve the technology. For example, Thomas Edison thought electric vehicles were the superior mode of transportation and worked to build a better battery.

- World's First Hybrid Electric Car is Invented (1901): Ferdinand Porsche, founder of the sports car by the same name, creates the Lohner Porsche Mixte -- the world's first hybrid electric car. The vehicle is powered by electricity stored in a battery and a gas engine.
- Model T Deals a Blow to Electric Vehicles (1908-1912): The mass-produced Model T makes gas-powered cars widely available and affordable. In 1912, the electric starter is introduced, helping to increase gas-powered vehicle sales even more.
- The decline in Electric Vehicles (1920 — 1935): Better roads and the discovery of cheap Texas crude oil helped contribute to the decline in electric vehicles.
- Gas Prices Soar (1960 — 1970): Cheap, abundant gasoline and continued improvement in the internal combustion engine created little need for alternative fuel vehicles. But in the 1960s and 1970s, gas prices soar through the roof, creating interest in electric vehicles again.
- Over the Moon with Electric Vehicles (1971): Around this same time, the first manned vehicle drives on the moon. NASA's lunar rover runs on electricity, helping to raise the profile of electric vehicles.
- The Next Generation of Electric Vehicles (1973): Many big and small automakers begin exploring options for alternative fuel vehicles. For example, General Motors develops a prototype for an urban electric car, which the company displayed at the First Symposium on Low Pollution Power Systems Development in 1973.
- Leader in Electric Vehicle Sales (1974 — 1977): One successful electric car at this time is Sebring-Vanguard's CitiCar. The company produces more than 2,000 CitiCars - wedge-shaped compact cars that had a range of 50-60 miles. Its popularity makes Sebring-Vanguard the sixth-largest U.S. automaker by 1975.
- Interest in Electric Cars Fades (1979): Compared to gas-powered cars, electric vehicles at this time have drawbacks, including limited performance and range, causing interest in electric cars to fade.
- New Regulations Renew Electric Vehicle Interest (1990 — 1992): New federal and state regulations create a renewed interest in electric vehicles. The result: Automakers begin modifying popular vehicle models into electric vehicles, enabling them to achieve speeds and performance much closer to gasoline-powered vehicles.
- EV1 (1996): GM releases the EV1, an electric vehicle that was designed and developed from the ground up.

- First Mass-Produced Hybrid (1997): Toyota introduces the first mass-produced hybrid, the Prius. In 2000, Toyota releases the Prius worldwide, and it becomes an instant success with celebrities, increasing its profile.
- Building a Better Electric Car (1999): Behind the scenes, scientists and engineers were working to improve electric vehicles and their batteries.
- Silicon Valley Startup Takes on Electric Cars (2006): Tesla Motors, a Silicon Valley startup, announces, that it will produce a luxury electric sports car with a range of 200+ miles. Other automakers take note, of accelerating work on their electric vehicles.
- Developing a Nation-Wide Charging Infrastructure (2009): To help consumers charge their vehicles on the go, charger installation started in various countries.
- First Commercially Available Plug-In Hybrid for Sale (2010): GM releases the Chevy Volt, making it the first commercially available plug-in hybrid.
- Nissan Launches the LEAF (2010): In December 2010, Nissan releases the LEAF, an all-electric, zero tailpipe emissions car.
- Electric Vehicle Battery Costs Drop (2013): The battery is the most expensive part of an electric vehicle. Battery costs drop by 50 percent in just four years, making electric vehicles more affordable for consumers.
- Electric Vehicles and a Multitude of Choices (2014): Consumers now have a multitude of choices when buying an electric vehicle, including hybrids, plug-in hybrids, and all-electric.
- Global Electric vehicle adoption: Many EV startups came into existence. Companies started manufacturing various EV Products ranging from 2 Wheeler, 3 Wheeler, 4 Wheeler, and Commercial Vehicles.

# VI
# EV Market

## Global EV Market

The global EV market is expected to grow from 8,151,000 units in 2022 to 39,208,000 units by 2030, with a CAGR of 21.7%. Increasing demand for low-emission commuting and factors such as the government supporting zero-emission long-haul vehicles through subsidies and tax cuts are forcing manufacturers to offer electric vehicles around the world. This has increased the demand for electric vehicles in the market. Countries around the world set emission reduction targets based on their capabilities.

Increasing government investment around the world in the development of electric vehicle charging stations and hydrogen fuel stations will create opportunities for OEMs to expand their revenue streams and geographic footprint, along with buyer incentives. The Asia-Pacific EV market is expected to grow steadily due to the high demand for low-cost, low-emission vehicles, while the North American and European markets are growing rapidly due to government initiatives and growth in the high-performance passenger car segment. A relatively less number of EV charging stations and hydrogen fuel stations, higher costs involved in initial investments, and performance constraints could hamper the growth of the global electric vehicle market.

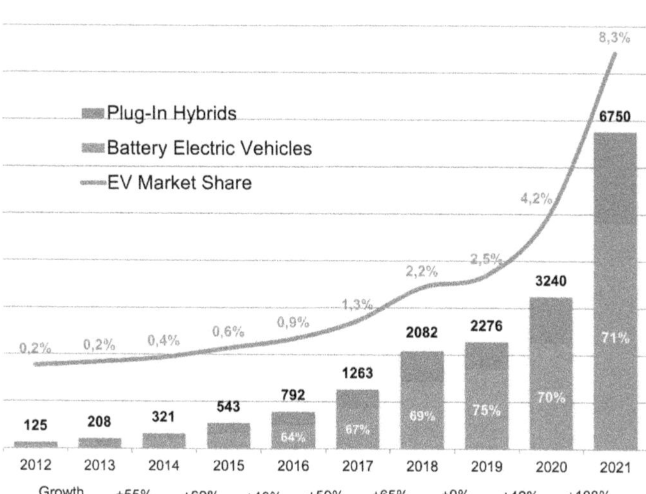


Figure 2 - Global EV Market

## Indian EV Market

India's electric vehicle market is valued at the US $ 1,434,040 million in 2021 and is projected to reach the US $ 15,397.9 billion by 2027, growing at a CAGR of 47.09% over the projected period (2022-2027). The COVID19 pandemic restricted domestic electric vehicles by losing manufacturing facilities. However, as regulations were relaxed, EVs grew brightly as consumers were drawn to affordable, environmentally-friendly transportation backed by government incentives. India's automotive sector is dominated by two-wheeled vehicles (scooters, motorcycles) and tricycles (cars and rickshaws), which play an important role in India's Lastmile mobility. Increasingly focus by the government to improve the country's EV ecosystem is resulting in partnerships between private and government stakeholders. Increased investment and product launches by major domestic OEMs and a focus on localization of supply chain facilities should ensure a positive market outlook.

In addition, the maturity of the Indian market varies from state to state depending on factors such as demographics, income levels, regulatory status, and urbanization. For example, Uttar Pradesh, which has the lowest urbanization rate, has a large adoption of electric motorcycles. On the other hand, Maharashtra has the highest penetration rate of passenger cars. Due to the high demand for electric buses and trucks, Delhi has the largest electric commercial vehicles.

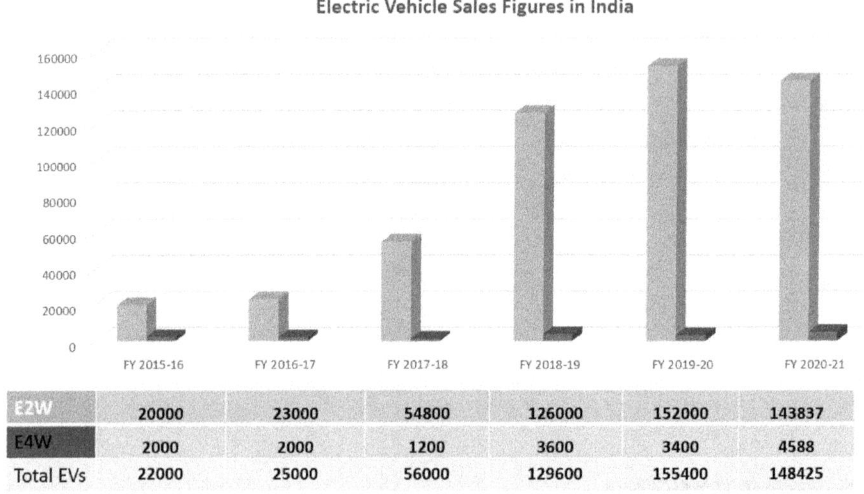


| | FY 2015-16 | FY 2016-17 | FY 2017-18 | FY 2018-19 | FY 2019-20 | FY 2020-21 |
|---|---|---|---|---|---|---|
| E2W | 20000 | 23000 | 54800 | 126000 | 152000 | 143837 |
| E4W | 2000 | 2000 | 1200 | 3600 | 3400 | 4588 |
| Total EVs | 22000 | 25000 | 56000 | 129600 | 155400 | 148425 |

Figure 3 - Indian EV Market

# VII
# EV Ecosystem

## Indian EV Industry

India has seen active progress in recent weeks, especially in electric vehicles (EVs). The main focus is on improving the country's EV capabilities and affordability. Currently, India's EV industry is still developing, with two main electric car manufacturers, a few commercial vehicle and bus manufacturers, and about a dozen motorcycle and tricycle manufacturers. Automakers, battery makers, suppliers, retailers, and utilities are having a hard time figuring out how to get all this to work on their own. However, an important requirement is for these stakeholders to unite and work with a single goal to create a sustainable EV ecosystem in the country. Codependence, partnerships, and alliances will be an encouraging outcome of EV development over the next few years. Several foreign cooperation and associations have already been established among OEMs, battery manufacturers, and other suppliers, and much more is expected in the future.

For the growth of EVs in India, the availability of important raw materials and technologies will play a crucial role. In terms of raw materials, India, like most other countries in the world, is currently importing the needs of battery-grade lithium, nickel, cobalt, and graphite, which are fundamental elements in the manufacture of rechargeable batteries. India needs to consider favorable trade agreements and memorandums of understanding with relevant countries to protect the supply and price of these commodities, especially given the rising international demand and therefore the competition for these resources. From a technical point of view, the manufacture of lithium batteries also requires appropriate and up-to-date technology transfer. Inadequate semiconductor manufacturing and inadequate knowledge of electronic control design are other pressing challenges. These branches form the main foundation for the operation of the hardware systems required for electric vehicles. Industrial policy needs to address the issues that drive their feasibility and growth for the development of the skills needed in the country.

## An ecosystem approach

Countries have set deadlines to reduce the production of internal combustion engine vehicles to achieve the goals set by the Paris Agreement. However, the share of the most practical alternative, the electric vehicle (EV), was only 4% of global vehicle sales in 2020. To accelerate adoption, EV manufacturers need to amplify the network effect of other stakeholders in the mobility ecosystem. Despite government regulation and financial support, electric vehicles face serious market obstacles. Adoption has been delayed due to high prices, limited scope, and lack of charging infrastructure. Fragmented solutions are unlikely to accelerate sales enough to reach ambitious country goals. An ecosystem approach is needed to drive the adoption of large EVs. This amplifies the value offered across manufacturers. That is the network effect of customers, charging stations, telecommunications and technology partners, and transportation providers throughout the ecosystem.

# VIII

# E-Mobility in India

India's history of electric vehicles began in the 19th century before REVA electric vehicles hit the market. REVA was the first electric vehicle to make a splash on the market. Before that, there were electric three-wheeled vehicles, electric buses, and small two-seater electric vehicles that were launched before REVA, but were abolished by companies due to sluggish sales and too many technical problems. In 1993, India's first electric vehicle was launched. In 1996, India's first electric tricycle was launched. In 2000, India's first electric bus was launched.

## Lovebird

India's first electric car was an electric car called a lovebird. Lovebird was founded by MD Jose and manufactured by Eddy Current Controls, a company based in Chalakkudy, Kerala. It was a cute two-seater that was popular with car enthusiasts at the time. It had a DC motor and a 4-speed gearbox. It had a range of 60km ago. It took 6-8 hours for the battery to fully charge. The car was first unveiled at the Delhi Auto Expo in 1993, after which the government allowed the commercial sale of lovebirds. However, they could only sell 25 cars, including institutional investors and individual buyers. In addition, the government stopped subsidies of Rs 80,000 and eventually ended the production of lovebirds. This is the end of lovebirds.

## Vikram Safa

In 1996, India's first electric tricycle, developed by Scooter's India Pvt Ltd., was launched. The tricycle was called "Vikram Safa". Approximately 400 vehicles were manufactured and sold, but because they were driven by lead-acid batteries, the batteries ran out every 41,250 kilometers, increasing running costs.

## Electric Bus by BHEL

In 2000, the first electric bus was developed by BHEL. It was an 18-seater electric bus powered by a lead-acid battery. About 200 of these buses were built and deployed in Delhi with the support of the Ministry of Non-Conventional Energy Sources. However, the problem with the bus was the high cost of the battery, short life, and poor consistency.

## REVA: India's first successful electric vehicle

After all, RECC launched REVA, India's first successful electric vehicle, in 2001. Reva Electric Car Company (RECC) was founded in 1994 by Chetan Maini, co-founder, and vice-chairman of Sun Mobility, as a joint venture between Maini Group in Bangalore and Amerigon Electric Vehicle Technologies (AEVT Inc.) in the United States. .. The company's sole goal was to develop and manufacture affordable compact electric vehicles.

## Acquisition of RECC by M & M

On May 26, 2010, Mahindra & Mahindra, India's largest SUV and tractor manufacturer, acquired a dominant 55.2% stake in Reva. After the acquisition, the company was renamed Mahindra Reva Electric Vehicles Private Limited. Mahindra's president of the automotive division, Pawang Nguyenka, has become chairman of the new company. In 2016 the company was renamed Mahindra Electric Mobility Ltd. It aims to reflect not only the business area of vehicle production but also the development of powertrain and integrated mobility solutions.

# IX

# India's electric vehicle journey

The concept of electric vehicles (EVs) has been around for quite some time but has only received a lot of attention over the last decade. Increased carbon dioxide emissions and the environmental impact of other fuels have led policymakers around the world to take electric vehicles seriously. In India, the central government has taken various steps to encourage more Indians to adopt electric vehicles.

- **November 2010:** The Manmohan Singh-led United Progressive Alliance government announced a scheme with an outlay of Rs 95 crore to incentivize electric vehicles. The scheme envisaged incentives of up to 20 percent on ex-factory prices of the vehicles, subject to a cap.

- **March 2012:** The Ministry of New & Renewable Energy (MNRE) discontinued the Rs 95-crore subsidy scheme causing a 70 percent drop in EV sales and temporary or permanent closure of several dealerships.

- **2013:** India unveiled National Electric Mobility Mission Plan (NEMMP) 2020 to make a major shift to electric vehicles and tackle national energy security, vehicle pollution, and domestic manufacturing capacity growth. The program provided grants and created a supporting infrastructure for electric vehicles.

- **2014:** In two years of the March 2012 discontinuation of subsidy on EVs, electric two-wheeler sales crashed to a mere 21,000 units a year. Electric two-wheeler makers were out of business due to poor demand.

- **2015:** To promote the sale of electric vehicles in the country, the government earmarked Rs 1,000 crore for the NEMMP for the next two financial years. The amount was to be used for setting up infrastructure, technology development, incentives, and pilot projects.

- **February 2015:** In the budget for 2015-16, then-Treasury Secretary Arun Jaitley allocated Rs 75 crore for the adoption and manufacturing acceleration (FAME) of electric vehicles. Electric Vehicle makers called this a good start.

- **December 2016:** The Central government's November 8 decision to demonetize high-value currency in circulation at the time hits sales of electric vehicles, which are mostly bought in cash transactions in the absence of a financing facility.

- **May 2017:** Automakers urged the government to lower a proposed sales tax of 43 percent on hybrid vehicles, as they feared the planned rate could make the development of the technology unviable.

- **July 2017:** Phase I of the FAME scheme, which was initially for two years from April 1, 2015, was extended for six months until September 30, 2017, with a slight modification. The benefits available to the Mild Hybrid technology under the scheme were discontinued from April 1, 2017.

- **February 2018:** Transport Minister Nitin Gadkari released a statement indicating India's intention to switch to 100% electric cars by 2030. Afterward, the government diluted its plans for electric passenger cars from 100 percent to 30 percent.

- **March 2018:** The second phase of the FAME scheme got delayed by six months. The delay was due to the lack of consensus among stakeholders within the government on the allocation of funds.

- **February 2019:** The Union Cabinet cleared the Rs 10,000-crore FAME II scheme for promoting electric vehicles.

- **July 2019:** The Goods and Services Tax (GST) council lowered the rate on EVs from 12 percent to 5 percent and on electric chargers from 18 percent to 5 percent. The rate cut gives a clear signal that the government proposes to forge ahead with its target of reducing urban pollution and crude oil import bill.

- **August 2019:** The Ministry of Heavy Industries, the Ministry of Road Transport and Highways, the power ministry, and the NITI Aayog — were tasked with policymaking and implementation of the government's e-mobility plan. Under the revised plan, highly-polluted urban cities were to be targeted first.

- **2020:** To push local manufacturing in the EV segment, govt had increased customs duty on imported completely built units (CBUs) of commercial EVs to 40 percent with effect from April 1, 2020.

- **September 2021:** A production-linked incentive scheme for the automotive sector was approved by the Cabinet to boost the manufacturing of electric vehicles and hydrogen fuel cell vehicles.

- **Feb 2022:** Union Budget for 2022-23 has reiterated the promotion of electric vehicles, as a means of transportation in the country. In addition to existing financial incentives under the FAME-II scheme (Rs. 10,000 crores) to boost demand and the PLI Schemes for ACC (Rs. 18,100 crores) & the auto segment focused on EVs / other alternative energy technologies (Rs. 25,938 crores), the finance minister in the Budget announced plans to implement a battery swapping policy and formalize interoperability standards.

# X

# Gasoline Vehicle

Gasoline vehicles and diesel vehicles are similar. Both use an internal combustion engine. Gasoline vehicles typically use a spark-ignition internal combustion engine instead of the compression ignition system used in diesel vehicles. In a spark ignition system, fuel is injected into the combustion chamber and combined with air. The air-fuel mixture is ignited by sparks from the spark plug. Gasoline is the most common transportation fuel. You might have noticed the numbers that distinguish the gas classifications when choosing the type of gas. Usually 87, 89, and 91. These are octane numbers. The octane number indicates how resistant the fuel type is to combustion under pressure. Pressure produces heat, so the more pressure you add, the hotter something gets. When the gas is sufficiently pressurized, the heat generated by the pressure causes the gasoline to burn. The higher the octane number, the more resistant the fuel is to self-ignition under pressure. This is important for high-performance high-pressure engines.

## *Major components of gasoline vehicles*

- **Battery:** The battery powers the engine to start and powers the vehicle's electronics/accessories.

- **Electronic control module (ECM):** The ECM controls the fuel mixture, ignition timing, and exhaust system; monitors the operation of the vehicle; safeguards the engine from abuse; and detects and troubleshoots problems.

- **Exhaust system:** The exhaust system sends the exhaust gas from the engine to the outside through the tail pipe. A three-way catalyst is designed to reduce engine-out emissions within the exhaust system.

- **Fuel Filler:** The fuel pump nozzle is attached to the vehicle's receptacle to fill the tank.

- **Fuel injection system:** This system introduces fuel into the combustion chamber of the engine for ignition.

- **Fuel line:** A metal tube or flexible hose carries fuel from the tank to the engine's fuel injection system.

- **Fuel pump:** A pump that pumps fuel from the tank through the fuel line to the fuel injection system of the engine.

- **Fuel Tank:** This tank stores gasoline in the vehicle until the engine needs it.

- **Internal Combustion Engine (Spark Ignition):** In this configuration, fuel is injected into either the intake manifold or the combustion chamber, where it is combined with air and then the air/fuel mixture is ignited by sparks from the spark plugs.

- **Transmission:** The transmission drives the wheels by transmitting mechanical power from an internal combustion engine.

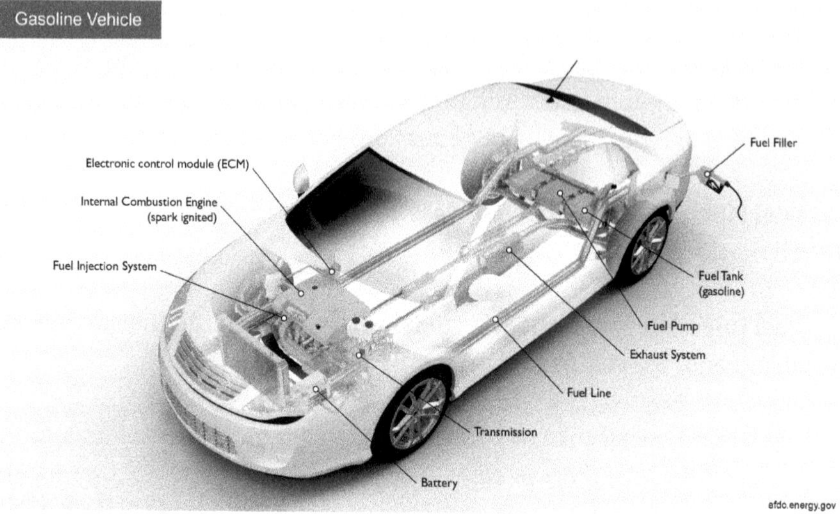


Figure 4 - Gasoline Vehicle

# XI
# Hybrid Electric Vehicle

Hybrid electric vehicles are driven by an internal combustion engine and one or more electric motors that use the energy stored in the battery. It is not possible to connect a hybrid electric vehicle to the charger for charging the battery. Instead, the battery is charged by regenerative braking and an internal combustion engine. The vehicle captures energy that is normally lost during braking by using the electric motor as a generator and storing the captured energy in the battery. The extra power provided by the electric motor can potentially assist engines. The battery also powers the auxiliary load and can also reduce engine idling when stopped. By combining these features, you can improve fuel economy without sacrificing performance. HEVs combine the benefits of high fuel consumption and low tailpipe emissions with the performance and range of traditional vehicles. Various HEV models are currently available. HEVs are often more expensive than comparable traditional vehicles, but some costs can be recovered through fuel savings and government incentives.

## *HEV Classification*

HEVs can be either mild or full hybrids, and full hybrids can be designed in series or parallel configurations.

- **Mild hybrids** (also known as micro-hybrid) use batteries and electric motors to propel the vehicle, allowing the engine to stop when the vehicle is stopped (such as at traffic lights or in stop-and-go traffic). Mild hybrid systems cannot drive a vehicle on electricity alone. These vehicles are generally cheaper than full hybrids but have less fuel economy benefits than full hybrids

- **Full hybrid** vehiclesare equipped with larger batteries and more powerful electric motors, allowing them to propel the vehicle over short distances and at low speeds. These vehicles cost more than mild hybrids, but they are more fuel-efficient.
- **Parallel hybrids** the most common HEV design—connects the engine and the electric motor to the wheels through mechanical coupling. Both the electric motor and the internal combustion engine drive the wheels directly.
- **Series hybrids** use only the electric motor to drive the wheels, which are more commonly found in plug-in hybrid electric vehicles.

## *Major components of hybrid electric vehicles*

- **Battery (Auxiliary Battery):** In electric vehicles, the low voltage auxiliary battery powers the vehicle to start before the traction battery is activated. It also powers vehicle accessories.
- **DC / DC Converter:** This device converts the high voltage DC power from the traction battery pack to the low voltage DC power needed to run vehicle accessories and charge the auxiliary battery.
- **Generator:** Generates electricity from the wheel rotation during the braking and returns this energy to the traction battery pack. Some vehicles use motor generators that perform both propulsion and regeneration functions.
- **Electric Traction Motor:** Using power from the traction battery pack, this motor drives the wheels of the vehicle. Some vehicles use motor generators that perform both propulsion and regeneration functions.

- **Exhaust system:** The exhaust system sends the exhaust gas from the engine to the outside through the tail pipe. A three-way catalyst is designed to reduce engine-out emissions within the exhaust system.

- **Fuel Filler:** The fuel pump nozzle is attached to the vehicle's receptacle to fill the tank.

- **Fuel Tank:** This tank stores gasoline in the vehicle until the engine needs it.

- **Internal Combustion Engine (Spark Ignition):** In this configuration, fuel is injected into either the intake manifold or the combustion chamber, where it is combined with air. And the air/fuel mixture is ignited by sparks from the spark plugs.

- **Power electronics controller:** This unit manages the flow of electrical energy from the traction battery to the motor and the speed/torque control of the electric traction motor.

- Thermal system (cooling): This system maintains a reasonable operating temperature range for engines, electric motors, power electronics, and other components.

- **Traction battery pack:** Stores electricity for use by the electric traction motor.

- **Transmission:** The transmission transfers mechanical power from the engine and/or electric traction motor to drive the wheels.

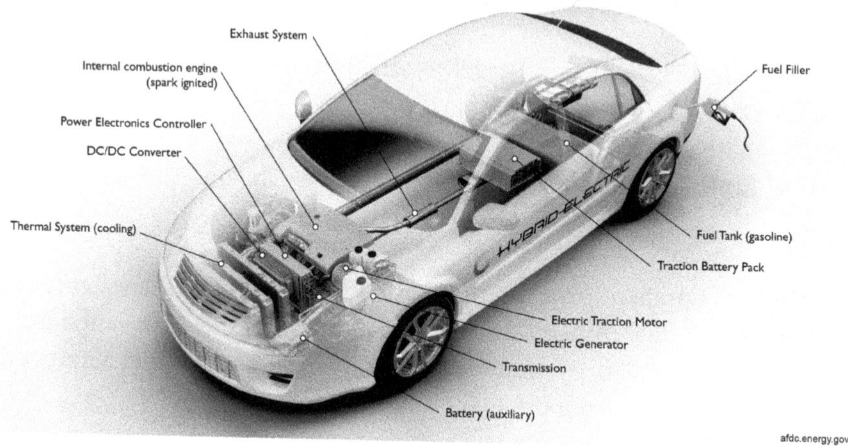


Figure 5 - Hybrid Electric Vehicle

# XII

# Plug-In Hybrid Electric Vehicle

Plug-in hybrid electric vehicles (PHEVs) use batteries to power electric motors and other fuels such as gasoline and diesel to power internal combustion engines. PHEVs can charge the battery via a charger and regenerative braking. Using power from the grid to drive the vehicle for some time or all the time reduces running costs and fuel consumption compared to traditional vehicles. PHEVs can also reduce emissions, depending on the power source and how often the vehicle is operated in pure electric mode. Several small PHEVs and medium-sized vehicles are currently on the market. Medium and large vehicles can also be converted to PHEVs. PHEVs are generally more expensive than similar traditional and hybrid vehicles, but some costs can be recovered through fuel savings, federal tax credits, or government incentives. The PHEV is equipped with an internal combustion engine and an electric motor that uses the energy stored in the battery. PHEVs generally have a larger battery pack than hybrid electric vehicles. This makes it possible to drive a reasonable distance (about 15-60 miles or more) with electricity alone, commonly referred to as the "Battery Range" of the vehicle. During urban driving, most of a PHEV's power can come from stored electricity. For example, a light-duty PHEV driver might drive to and from work on all-electric power, plug the vehicle in to charge at night, and be ready for another all-electric commute the next day. The internal combustion engine powers the vehicle when the battery is mostly depleted, during rapid acceleration, or when intensive heating or air conditioning loads are present. Some heavy-duty PHEVs work the opposite way, with the internal combustion engine used for driving to and from a job site and the battery used to power the vehicle's auxiliary equipment or control the cab's climate while at the job site.

PHEV batteries can be charged by an external power source, internal combustion engine, or regenerative braking. When braked, the electric motor acts as a generator and uses that energy to charge the battery and recover the lost energy. PHEV fuel consumption depends on the distance driven between battery charges. For example, if the vehicle is never plugged in to charge, fuel economy will be about the same as a similarly sized hybrid electric vehicle. If the vehicle is driven a shorter distance than its all-electric range and plugged in to charge between trips, it may be possible to use only battery power. Therefore, consistently charging the vehicle is the best way to maximize the electric benefits.

In addition to battery and engine output, there are various ways to combine the output of an electric motor and combustion engine. The two main configurations are parallel and serial. Some PHEVs operate in parallel or series configurations and use a transmission that can switch between the two based on the propulsion profile.

- **Parallel hybrid** operation connects the internal combustion engine and electric motor to the wheels via a mechanical coupling. Both electric motors and combustion engines can drive the wheels directly.

- **Series plug-in hybrids** use only electric motors to drive the wheels. Internal combustion engines are used to generate electricity for motors. This type of vehicle is often referred to as an extended-range electric vehicle. Electric motors always drive the wheels, but when the battery is dead, the vehicle can behave like a parallel hybrid.

## *Major components of plug-In hybrid electric vehicles*

- **Battery (Auxiliary Battery):** In electric vehicles, the low voltage auxiliary battery powers the vehicle to start before the traction battery is activated. It also powers vehicle accessories.

- **Charging Port:** The charging port allows you to connect your vehicle to an external power source to charge your traction battery pack.

- **DC / DC Converter:** This device converts the high voltage DC power from the traction battery pack to the low voltage DC power needed to run vehicle accessories and charge the auxiliary battery.

- **Generator:** Generates electricity from wheel rotation during braking and returns this energy to the traction battery pack. Some vehicles use motor generators that perform both propulsion and regeneration functions.

- **Electric Traction Motor:** Using power from the traction battery pack, this motor drives the wheels of the vehicle. Some vehicles use motor generators that perform both propulsion and regeneration functions.

- **Exhaust system:** The exhaust system sends the exhaust gas from the engine to the outside through the tail pipe. The three-way catalytic converter is designed to reduce emissions from the engine in the exhaust system.

- **Fuel Filler:** The fuel pump nozzle is attached to the vehicle's receptacle to fill the tank.

- **Fuel Tank (Gasoline):** This tank stores gasoline in the vehicle until the engine needs it.

- **Internal Combustion Engine (Spark Ignition):** In this configuration, fuel is injected into either the intake manifold or the combustion chamber, where it is combined with air. And the air/fuel mixture is ignited by sparks from the spark plugs.

- **Onboard Charger:** Takes the AC power supplied from the charging port and converts it to DC power to charge the traction battery. It also communicates with the charging device to monitor battery characteristics such as voltage, current, temperature, and charge status while the battery is charging.

- **Power Electronics Control:** This unit manages the flow of electrical energy from the traction battery to the motor and the speed/torque control of the electric traction motor.

- **Thermal system (cooling):** This system maintains a reasonable operating temperature range for engines, electric motors, power electronics, and other components.

- **Traction Battery Pack:** Stores electricity for use.

- **Transmission:** The transmission drives the wheels by transmitting mechanical power from an internal combustion engine and/or an electric traction motor.

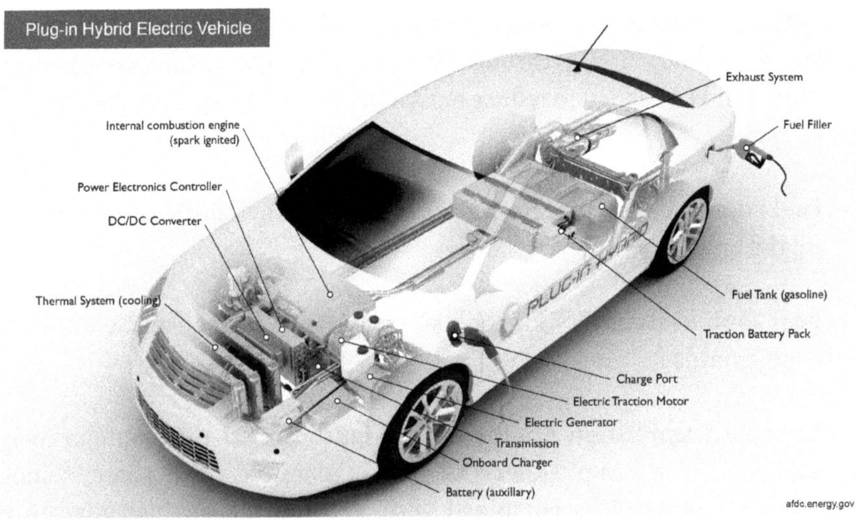


Figure 6 - Plug-In Hybrid Electric Vehicle

# XIII

# Battery Electric Vehicle

All-electric vehicles, also known as battery-powered electric vehicles (BEVs), use battery packs to store the electrical energy that powers the motors. The battery is charged by connecting the vehicle to a power source. Power generation can contribute to air pollution, but the US Environmental Protection Agency classifies pure electric vehicles as zero-emission vehicles because they do not generate direct or tailpipe emissions. Both large and lightweight all-electric vehicles are commercially available. BEVs are usually more expensive than similar traditional and hybrid vehicles, but the costs can be recovered through fuel savings, federal tax credits, or government incentives. Pure electric vehicles today generally have a shorter range (per charge) than comparable conventional vehicles. However, this gap is narrowing due to the expansion of the range of new models and the further development of high-performance chargers. The efficiency and range of BEVs will vary greatly depending on operating conditions. Extreme outside temperatures tend to narrow the range, as more energy is required to heat or cool the cabin. Fully electric vehicles are more efficient in urban traffic than when driving on the highway. Rapid acceleration reduces the range of the vehicle compared to slow acceleration. Towing heavy loads or climbing steep hills can shorten your range.

## *Major components of battery electric vehicles*

- **Battery (All Electric Auxiliary Battery):** In EV, the auxiliary battery powers the vehicle's accessories.

- **Charging Port:** The charging port allows you to connect your vehicle to an external power source to charge your traction battery pack.

- **DC / DC Converter:** This device converts the high voltage DC power from the traction battery pack to the low voltage DC power needed to run vehicle accessories and charge the auxiliary battery.

- **Electric Traction Motor:** Using power from the traction battery pack, this motor drives the wheels of the vehicle. Some vehicles use motor generators that perform both propulsion and regeneration functions.

- **Onboard Charger:** Takes the AC power supplied from the charging port and converts it to DC power to charge the traction battery. It also communicates with the charging device to monitor battery characteristics such as voltage, current, temperature, and charge status while the battery is charging.

- **Power Electronics Control:** This unit manages the flow of electrical energy from the traction battery to the motor and the speed/torque control of the electric traction motor.

- **Thermal system (cooling):** This system maintains a reasonable operating temperature range for electric motors, power electronics, and other components.

- **Traction Battery Pack:** Stores electricity for electric traction motors.

- **Transmission (Electric):** The transmission drives the wheels by transmitting mechanical power from an electric traction motor.

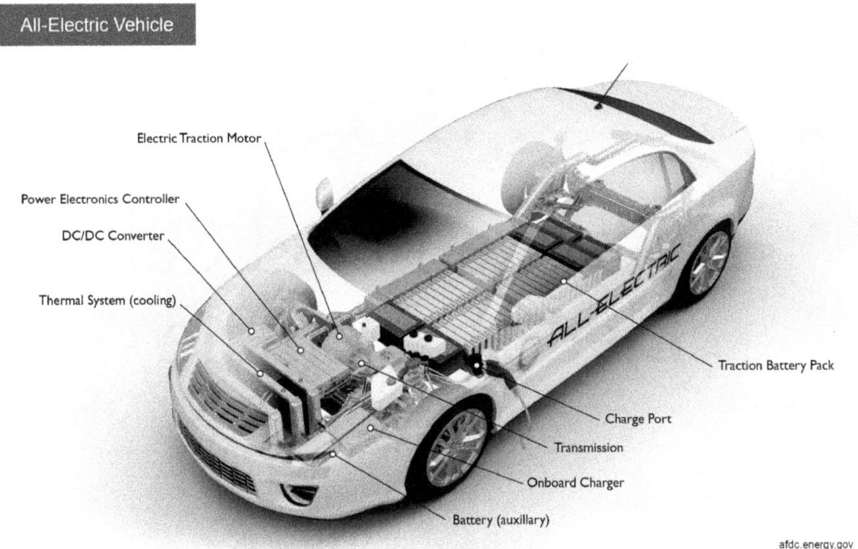


Figure 7 - Battery Electric Vehicle

# XIV

# Hydrogen Fuel Cell Electric Vehicle

Fuel cell electric vehicles (FCEVs) run on hydrogen. They are more efficient than traditional internal combustion engine vehicles and do not generate emissions from the tailpipe. It only discharges water vapor and warm air. Various government departments are leading research efforts to make hydrogen-powered vehicles an affordable, environmentally friendly, and safe transportation option. Hydrogen is considered an alternative fuel. FCEV uses a propulsion system similar to that of an electric vehicle, and the energy stored as hydrogen is converted into electricity by a fuel cell. Unlike traditional internal combustion engine vehicles, these vehicles do not produce harmful tailpipe emissions. Other benefits include increased energy resilience and better economics. FCEVs operate on pure hydrogen gas stored in vehicle tanks. Like a traditional internal combustion engine vehicle, it can be refueled in less than 4 minutes and has a range of over 300 miles. FCEVs are equipped with other advanced technologies to increase efficiency. Major automobile manufacturers are offering a limited but growing number of FCEVs to the public in certain markets, in sync with what the developing infrastructure can support.

## *Major components of hydrogen fuel cell electric vehicle*

**Battery (Auxiliary Battery):** In electric vehicles, the low voltage auxiliary battery powers the vehicle to start before the traction battery is activated. It also powers vehicle accessories.

**Battery pack:** This high voltage battery stores the energy generated by regenerative braking and supplies additional power to the electric traction motor.

**DC / DC Converter:** This device converts the high voltage DC power from the traction battery pack to the low voltage DC power needed to run vehicle accessories and charge the auxiliary battery.

**Electric Traction Motor (FCEV):** Using power from fuel cells and traction battery packs, this motor drives the wheels of the vehicle. Some vehicles use motor generators that perform both propulsion and regeneration functions.

**Fuel cell stack:** An assembly of individual membrane electrodes that use hydrogen and oxygen to generate electricity.

**Fuel Filler:** The fuel pump nozzle is attached to the vehicle's receptacle to fill the tank.

**Fuel tank (hydrogen):** Stores hydrogen gas in the vehicle until it is needed by the fuel cell.

**Power Electronics Controller (FCEV):** This unit controls the flow of electrical energy provided by the fuel cell and traction battery, controlling the speed of the electric traction motor and the torque it produces.

**Thermal System (Cooling) (FCEV):** This system maintains a reasonable operating temperature range for fuel cells, electric motors, power electronics, and other components.

**Transmission (Electric):** The transmission drives the wheels by transmitting mechanical power from an electric traction motor.

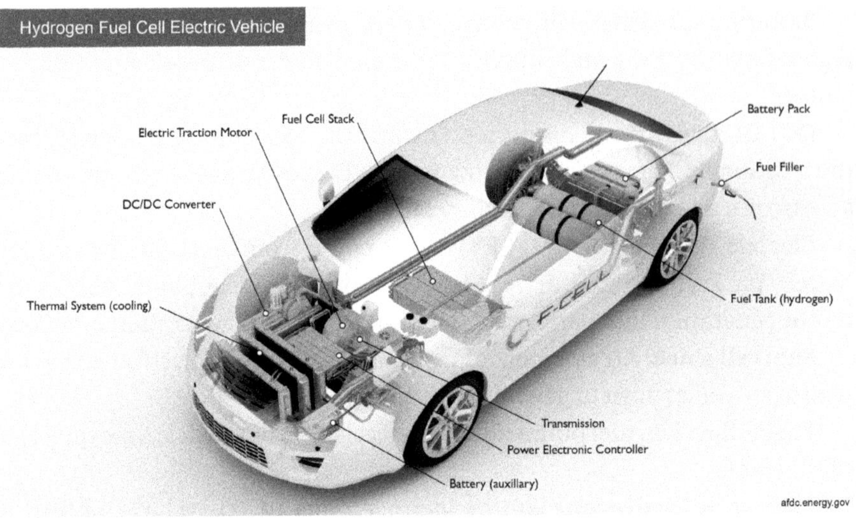


Figure 8 - Hydrogen Fuel Cell Electric Vehicle

# XV

# Motors for Electric Vehicle

Electric vehicles are nothing new in the world, but they are tagged for future mobility due to technological advances and growing interest in pollution control. The core element of an electric vehicle is the electric motor, which replaces the internal combustion engine. Rapid development in the field of power electronics and control technology has created space for different types of electric motors that can be used in electric vehicles. Electric motors in automotive applications must-have characteristics such as high starting torque, high power density, and excellent efficiency. Much has happened in this field since the invention of the motor, making it a very important topic for modern engineers.

## An electric motor history:

In 1821, British scientist Michael Faraday defined the conversion of electrical electricity into mechanical electricity by keeping a current-carrying conductor in a magnetic field. This caused the conductor to rotate due to the torque generated by the interaction of the current and the magnetic field. Based on his principles, the most primitive DC machine of all machines was designed in 1832 by another British scientist, William Sturgeon. However, his model was too expensive to be used for practical purposes. In late 1886, the first electric motor was invented by scientist Frank Julian Sprague. This allowed it to rotate at a constant speed over a wide range of loads.

## An electric motor:

An electric motor is an electric machine that converts electrical energy into mechanical energy. Most electric motors operate through the interaction between the motor's magnetic field and electric current in a wire winding. This interaction produces a force (according to Faraday's law) in the form of torque applied to the motor shaft. Electric motors can be powered by direct current (DC) power sources such as batteries and rectifiers. Or via alternating current (AC) power sources such as inverters, generators, and power grids.

## Motor principle

The basic principle underlying the functioning of an electrical motor is Faraday's Law of induction. Faraday's law of electromagnetic induction (called Faraday's law) is the basic law of electromagnetism that predicts how a magnetic field interacts with an electrical circuit to generate an electromotive force (EMF). This phenomenon is called electromagnetic induction.

**Faraday's law** states that an electric current is induced in a conductor exposed to a changing magnetic field.

**Lenz's law** of electromagnetic induction states that the direction of this induced current will be such that the magnetic field created by the induced current opposes the initial changing magnetic field which produced it.

Whenever a current-carrying conductor comes under a magnetic field, there will be a force acting on the conductor. The direction of this force can be found using **Fleming's Left Hand Rule.**

Similarly, if a conductor is forcefully brought under a magnetic field, there will be an induced current in that conductor. The direction of this force can be found using **Fleming's Right-Hand Rule.**

## Motor working:

**DC Motor**: The working principle of DC Motor mainly depends upon the Fleming Left-Hand rule. In a basic DC motor, an armature is placed in between magnetic poles. If the armature winding is supplied by an external DC source, current starts flowing through the armature conductors. As the conductors are carrying current inside a magnetic field, they will experience a force that tends to rotate the armature.

**AC Motor:** Working of the electric motor in the case of the AC motor is a little bit different from DC motor. In a single-phase induction motor, when a single-phase supply is given to the stator winding, a pulsating magnetic field is produced, and in a three-phase induction motor, when a three-phase supply is given to the three-phase stator winding, a rotating magnetic field is produced.

## Motor Types:

There are different types of motors that have been developed for different purposes. DC motors, as the name implies, are motors that operate on DC power. This is the most primitive version of an electric motor, where torque is generated by the current flowing through a conductor in a magnetic field. AC electric motors are driven by alternating currents. The synchronous motor always operates at synchronous speed. The induction motor, which is also known as the asynchronous motor, operates at slower speeds than synchronous speeds.

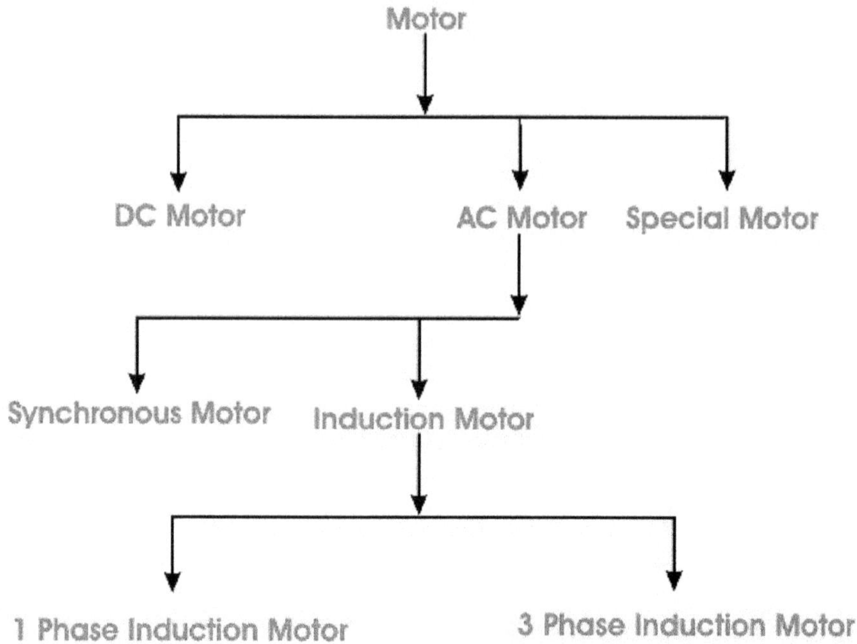


Figure 9 - Types of Motors

## Types of Electric Motors used in Electric Vehicles

1. DC Series Motor.
2. Brushless DC Motor.
3. Permanent Magnet Synchronous Motor (PMSM).
4. Three Phase AC Induction Motors.
5. Switched Reluctance Motors (SRM).

### *1. DC Series Motor:*

The DC Series Motor is similar to any other motor because the main function of this motor is to convert electrical energy to mechanical energy.

The high starting torque of the DC Series motors makes it a suitable option for traction applications. It was the most widely used motor in traction applications in the early 1900s.

**Advantages:**

- Vast starting torque.
- Easy assembly and simple design.
- Protection is easy.
- Cost-effective.

**Disadvantages:**

- High maintenance is required for brushes and commutators.
- Speed regulation in the series motor is quite poor.
- With the increase in speed, the torque of the dc series motor drops sharply.
- DC series motor should always require being loaded before starting the motor.

## 2. *Brushless DC Motor*

BLDC Motor stands for Brush Less DC motor, it is commonly used in Electric Vehicles due to its smooth operation. Although BLDC motors are considered to be DC motors, they work with the help of Pulsed waves. The Electronic speed controller (ESC) converts the DC voltage from the battery into pulses and provides it to the 3 wires of the Motor. It is called brushless because it does not have a commutator and brush arrangement. The commutation is done electronically in this motor because of this BLDC motors are maintenance-free.

BLDC motors further have two types:

**Out-runner type BLDC Motor:**

This type of motor has a rotor on the outside and a stator on the inside. It is also known as a hub motor because the wheels are directly connected to the outer rotor. These types of motors do not require an external gear system. In some cases, the motor itself has planetary gears built into it and does not require a transmission system, thus reducing the bulk of the entire vehicle. It also eliminates the space required for mounting the motor.

This motor is widely favored by electric bike manufacturers. It is used by motorcycle manufacturers also.

**In-runner type BLDC Motor:**

This type of motor has the rotor on the inside and the stator on the outside, similar to traditional motors. These motors require an external transmission system to transmit power to the wheels. For this reason, the outrunner configuration is a bit bulkier than the in-runner configuration. Many tricycle manufacturers use BLDC In-runner motors. Manufacturers of low and medium-power scooters also use BLDC In-runner motors for propulsion.

**Advantages:**

- Maintenance-free.
- Traction characteristics like high starting torque, high efficiency around 95-98%, etc.
- BLDC motors are suitable for a high power density design approach.

**Disadvantages:**

- The cost of a brushless DC motor is comparatively higher compared to a brushed DC motor.
- Wiring and operation of the motor are not that simple
- Resonance issue.

## *3. Permanent Magnet Synchronous Motor (PMSM)*

This motor is also similar to a BLDC motor with a permanent magnet in the rotor. Like BLDC motors, these motors have traction characteristics such as high output density and high efficiency. The difference is that PMSM has sinusoidal back EMF whereas BLDC has trapezoidal back EMF. Permanent magnet synchronous motors are available for higher power ratings. PMSM is ideal for high-power applications such as automobiles and buses. Despite the high cost, PMSMs are more efficient than induction motors, which makes them more competitive with induction motors. PMSMs are more expensive than BLDC motors. Most automakers use PMSM motors in their hybrid and electric vehicles.

**Advantages:**

- Higher efficiency than Brushless DC Motors.
- No torque ripple when the motor is commutated.
- Higher torque and better performance.
- More reliable and less noisy, than other asynchronous motors.
- High performance in both high and low-speed operation.
- Low rotor inertia makes it easy to control.
- Efficient dissipation of heat.
- Reduced size of the motor.

**Disadvantages:**

- Permanent magnet synchronous motors require a drive.
- Complex control system.
- Cost is Higher.

## *4. Three Phase AC Induction Motor*

Induction motors are commonly used AC electric motors. In induction motors, the current required to generate torque in the rotor is obtained from the rotating magnetic field of the stator windings via electromagnetic induction. The rotor of an induction motor can be a squirrel-cage or winding rotor. Induction motors do not have the high starting torque of DC series motors when operating at fixed voltages and frequencies. However, this property can be modified by various control techniques such as FOC and v / f methods. These control methods provide maximum torque suitable for traction applications when starting the motor. Squirrel-cage induction motors have a long life because they require less maintenance. Asynchronous motors can be designed with efficiency up to 92-95%. In permanent magnet motors, the magnets contribute to the flux density B. Therefore, adjusting the value of B in induction motors is easy when compared to permanent magnet motors. It is because in Induction motors the value of B can be adjusted by varying the voltage and frequency (V/f) based on torque requirements. This helps in reducing the losses which in turn improves the efficiency.

**Advantages:**

- Cheap cost compared to the other motors.

- Highly efficient motor.
- The maintenance is very less compared to the DC motor and synchronous motor.
- The working of an induction motor is very simple and unique.
- The construction of an induction motor is robust and also sturdy.
- Only the AC source requires to operate. It does not require DC excitation like the use of a synchronous motor.
- The speed variation from no load to rated load is very less.
- The induction motor is famous for its durability.
- It can also be operated in hazardous conditions.
- 3 phase induction motor has high starting torque, good speed regulation, and also reasonable overload capacity.

**Disadvantages:**

- During light load conditions, it operates at a very low power factor.
- The change in the speed of the motor is very low loading under different loading conditions, so the speed control of IM is difficult.
- 3-phase induction motors have poor starting torque and high inrush currents.

## *5. Switched Reluctance Motors (SRM)*

Switched reluctance motor works based on the variable reluctance principle. The rotating magnetic field is created with the help of power electronics switching circuit. The main concept is the reluctance of the magnetic circuit is depending on the air gap. Hence, by changing the air gap between the rotor and stator, we can change the reluctance of the motor. Switch reluctance motors are a category of variable reluctance motors with dual characteristics. The switch reluctance motor has a simple and robust structure. SRM rotors are laminated steel without windings or permanent magnets. This reduces the inertia of the rotor and contributes to high acceleration. The robustness of SRM makes it suitable for high-speed applications. SRM also provides high power density, which is some of the characteristics required for electric vehicles. The heat generated is primarily limited to the stator, which makes it easier to cool the motor.

**Advantages:**

- It does not require an external ventilation system.
- Available at a cheaper price.
- A simple three or two-phase pulse generator is enough to drive the motor.
- The direction of the motor can be reversed by changing the phase sequence.
- Self-starting (Does not require external arrangements)
- Starting torque can be very high without excessive inrush currents.
- High Fault Tolerance.
- Phase losses do not affect motor operations.
- High torque/inertia ratio.
- High starting torque can be achieved.

**Disadvantages:**

- Creates Torque ripple at high-speed operation.
- The external rotor position sensor is required.
- The noise level is high.
- At a higher speed, the motor generates harmonics.
- Since the absence of a Permanent Magnet, the motor has to be designed to carry a high input current. It increases the converter KVA requirement.

## Motor Selection for Electric Vehicles

Choosing the right electric motor for a particular vehicle is not always easy. With so many variables to consider, it can be difficult to know where to start. Below are 10 things that must be considered while selecting the motor for an electric vehicle:

1) Application of Motor (2 Wheeler/3 Wheeler/ 4 Wheeler /Other).
2) Motor Type (AC/DC).
3) Motor Power (Unit: W or kW).
4) Motor Voltage (Unit: V).
5) Motor RPM.
6) Motor Torque (Unit: Nm).
7) Performance (Power-Torque-RPM Curve).
8) Size (Dimensions).
9) Warranty/Guarantee/Service.

10) Cost.

# XVI
# Batteries for Electric Vehicles

Energy storage systems (batteries) are essential for pure electric vehicles (BEV), plug-in hybrid electric vehicles (PHEVs), and hybrid electric vehicles (HEVs).

## Types of Energy Storage Systems

### *Lithium-ion battery:*

Lithium-ion batteries are currently used in most portable home appliances such as mobile phones and laptops because of their high energy per unit mass compared to other electrical energy storage systems. In addition, the power-to-weight ratio is high, energy efficiency is high, high-temperature performance is high, and self-discharge is low. These characteristics of Lithium-Ion Batteries make them more suitable for EV application. Most lithium-ion battery components can be recycled, but the cost of material recovery remains a challenge for the industry. All-electric vehicles (BEV) and PHEVs today use lithium-ion batteries, but their exact chemistry is often different from that of household appliances. Research and development are underway to reduce relatively high costs, extend service life, and address safety concerns.

| Chemistry | Specific Energy | Voltage at 50% SOC | Life | Safety | Cost |
|---|---|---|---|---|---|
| LFP | 160 Ah/kg | 3.4 V | High | High | Medium |
| LMO | 100-200 Ah/kg | 4 V | Low | Medium | Low |
| LCO | 155 Ah/kg | 3.9 V | Medium | Low | Medium |
| NCA | 180 Ah/kg | 3.7 V | Medium | Low | High |
| NMC | 160 Ah/kg | 3.8 V | High | Medium | High |

Table 2 - Li-Ion Battery Chemistries

## *Nickel metal hydride battery:*

Nickel-metal hydride batteries, which are routinely used in computers and medical devices, provide the right specific energy and capacity. Nickel-metal hydride batteries have a much longer lifespan than lead-acid batteries and are safe and abuse-resistant. These batteries are widely used in HEVs. The main challenges of nickel-metal hydride batteries are high cost, high self-discharge, high-temperature heat generation, and the need to control hydrogen loss.

## *Lead-acid battery*

Lead-acid batteries can be designed for high performance, and are cheap, safe, and reliable. However, their use is hampered by a low specific energy, inadequate freezing capacity, and short calendars and life cycles. High-performance lead-acid batteries have been developed, but these batteries are only used in commercial electric vehicles for auxiliary loads.

## *Ultracapacitor*

Ultracapacitors store energy in a polarized liquid between the electrodes and the electrolyte. The energy storage capacity increases as the surface area of the liquid increases. Ultracapacitors provide additional power to the vehicle as it accelerates and climbs hills and helps restore braking energy. They are also useful as secondary energy storage devices for electric vehicles.

## Battery Management System

A battery management system (BMS) is technology dedicated to the oversight of a battery pack, which is an assembly of battery cells, electrically organized in a row x column matrix configuration to enable the delivery of a targeted range of voltage and current for a duration of time against expected load scenarios.

**The monitoring provided by BMS usually includes the following:**

- Monitoring the battery.
- Providing battery protection.
- Estimating the battery`s operational state.
- Continually optimizing battery performance.
- Reporting operational status to external devices.

Here, the term "battery" implies the entire pack; however, the monitoring and control functions are specifically applied to individual cells, or groups of cells called modules in the overall battery pack assembly. Lithium-ion rechargeable cells have the highest energy density and are the standard choice for battery packs for many consumer products, from laptops to electric vehicles. While they perform superbly, they can be rather unforgiving if operated outside a generally tight safe operating area (SOA), with outcomes ranging from compromising the battery performance to outright dangerous consequences. The BMS certainly has a challenging job description, and its overall complexity and oversight outreach may span many disciplines such as electrical, digital, control, thermal, and hydraulic.

Battery management systems have no fixed or clear standards that need to be adopted. The scope of technology design and the features implemented generally correlate with:

- Battery pack cost.
- Battery pack complexity & size.
- Battery usage and safety (Life and warranty concerns).
- Certification requirements from various government regulations that prioritize costs and penalties when functional safety measures are inadequate.

There are many BMS functions. Battery pack protection management and capacity management are two important functions.

## Electrical management protection: Current

Monitoring battery pack current and cell or module voltage is the path to electrical protection. The electrical SOA of each battery cell is limited by current and voltage. A well-designed BMS protects the pack by preventing it from operating outside the manufacturer's cell ratings. In many cases, you can apply more deratings to stay within the SOA safe zone to extend battery life. Battery cell manufacturers typically specify maximum continuous charge and discharge current limits and peak charge and discharge current limits. BMS that provides current protection reliably applies maximum continuous current. However, this can be preceded to account for sudden changes in load conditions. For example, the rapid acceleration of electric vehicles. A BMS may incorporate peak current monitoring by integrating the current and after delta time, deciding to either reduce the available current or break the pack current altogether. This allows the BMS to possess nearly instantaneous sensitivity to extreme current peaks, such as a short-circuit condition that has not caught the attention of any resident fuses but also be forgiving to high peak demands, as long as they are not excessive for too long.

## Electrical Management Protection: Voltage

Lithium-ion batteries must operate within a certain voltage range. Ultimately, these SOA limits are determined by the inherent chemistry of the selected lithium-ion battery and the temperature of the battery at any given time. In addition, these SOA voltage limits are usually further limited to optimize battery life, as each battery pack experiences a heavy power cycle, discharge due to load demand, and charging from various energy sources. BMS needs to know what these limits are and command decisions based on its proximity to these thresholds. For example, BMS may require that the charging current be gradually reduced as the high voltage limit is approached, or that the charging current is completely stopped when the limit is reached. However, this limitation usually comes with additional intrinsic voltage hysteresis considerations to prevent control chattering near the turn-off threshold. On the other hand, as the low voltage limit approaches, a BMS will request that key active offending loads reduce their current demands. For electric vehicles, this can be done by reducing the allowable torque available to the traction motor. Of course, BMS should put the safety aspect of the driver first while protecting the battery to avoid permanent damage.

## Thermal Management Protection: Temperature

The operating temperature range of lithium-ion batteries seems to be wide, but the speed of chemical reactions is significantly slowed down, which reduces the overall battery capacity at low temperatures. In terms of low-temperature performance, it is far superior to lead-acid batteries and NiMh batteries. However, charging below 0 ° C (32 ° F) is physically problematic and requires careful temperature control. The phenomenon of metallic lithium plating can occur at the anode during sub-zero charging. This is permanent damage that not only reduces capacity but is also prone to cell failure when exposed to vibrations and other stressful conditions. BMS can control the temperature of the battery pack by heating and cooling.

Thermal management is entirely dependent upon the size and cost of the battery pack, performance objectives, design criteria of the BMS, and product unit. Geographical consideration is another important consideration for Battery. It is generally more effective to draw energy from an external AC power source, or an alternative resident battery purposed to operate the heater when needed. However, if the electric heater has a low current draw, energy from the primary battery pack can be siphoned to heat itself. In a thermal-hydraulic system, an electric heater is used to heat the coolant which is pumped and distributed throughout the pack assembly.

Cooling is particularly important to minimize the performance loss of a lithium-ion battery pack. For example, a given battery operates optimally at 20°C; if the pack temperature increases to 30°C, its performance efficiency could be reduced by as much as 20%. If the pack is continuously charged and recharged at 45°C (113°F), the performance loss can rise to a hefty 50%. Battery life can also suffer from premature aging and degradation if continually exposed to excessive heat generation, particularly during fast charging and discharging cycles. Cooling is usually achieved by two methods, passive or active, and both techniques may be employed. Passive cooling relies on the movement of airflow to cool the battery. In the case of an electric vehicle, this implies that it is simply moving down the road. However, it may be more sophisticated than it appears, as airspeed sensors could be integrated to strategically auto-adjust deflective air dams to maximize airflow. Implementation of an active temperature-controlled fan can help at low speeds or when the vehicle has stopped, but all this can do is merely equalize the pack with the surrounding ambient temperature. In the event of a scorching hot day, this could increase the initial pack temperature. Thermal hydraulic active cooling can be designed, typically utilizing ethylene-glycol coolant with a specified mixture ratio, circulated via an electric motor-driven pump through pipes/hoses, distribution manifolds, and a cross-flow heat exchanger (radiator), and cooling plate resident against the battery pack assembly. A BMS monitors the temperatures across the pack, and opens and closes various valves to maintain the temperature of the overall battery within a narrow temperature range to ensure optimal battery performance.

## Capacity Management

Maximizing the capacity of the battery pack is one of the most important battery performance characteristics provided by BMS. If this maintenance is not performed, a battery pack may eventually render itself useless. The root of the issue is leakage or self-discharge. Leakage is not a manufacturer defect but a battery chemistry characteristic, though it may be statistically impacted by minute manufacturing process variations. Initially, a battery pack may have well-matched cells, but over time, the cell-to-cell similarity further degrades, not just due to self-discharge, but also impacted by charge/discharge cycling, elevated temperature, and general calendar aging. Once fully charged, cells cannot accept any more current, and any additional energy pushed into them gets transmuted into heat, with voltage potentially rising quickly, possibly to dangerous levels. It is not a healthy situation for the cell and can cause permanent damage and unsafe operating conditions if it continues. The battery pack series cell array is what determines the overall pack voltage, and mismatch between adjacent cells creates a dilemma when attempting to charge up any stack.

If you have a set of perfectly balanced cells, then each is charged evenly and can cut off the charging current when the upper limit cutoff threshold of 4.0 volts is reached. However, in the unbalanced scenario, the top cell will reach its charge limit early, and the charging current needs to be terminated for the leg before other underlying cells have been charged to full capacity. BMS intervenes and saves the battery pack. The charge state (SOC) of a cell or module at any given time is proportional to the available charge relative to the total charge when fully charged. Therefore, a 50% SOC battery means that it is 50% charged. BMS capacity management is to smooth out SOC fluctuations across each stack of packaging assemblies. SOC is not a directly measurable quantity and can be estimated by a variety of methods. The balancing scheme itself generally falls into two main categories: passive and active. There are many variations of themes, each with its strengths and weaknesses. It is the BMS designer's responsibility to determine the best for a particular battery pack and its application. Passive balancing is the easiest to implement, as well as to explain the general balancing concept. The passive method allows every cell in the stack to have the same charged capacity as the weakest cell. Using a relatively low current, it shuttles a small amount of energy from high SOC cells during the charging cycle so that all cells charge to their maximum SOC. It monitors each cell and leverages a transistor switch and an appropriately sized discharge resistor in parallel with each cell. When the BMS senses a given cell is approaching its charge limit, it will steer excess current around it to the next cell below in a top-down fashion.

A BMS balances a battery stack by allowing a cell or module in a stack to see a different charging current than the pack current in one of the following ways:

- Removal of charge from the most charged cells, which gives headroom for additional charging current to prevent overcharging, and allows the less charged cells to receive more charging current.
- Redirection of some or nearly all of the charging current around the most charged cells, thereby allowing the less charged cells to receive charging current for a longer length of time.

## Types of Battery Management Systems

Battery management systems range from simple to complex and can incorporate a variety of technologies to meet the core policy of "care for the battery." However, these systems can be categorized based on topology.

**Centralized BMS Architecture**

The battery pack assembly has a central BMS. All battery packs are directly connected to the central BMS. Centralized BMS has several advantages. Since there is only one BMS, it tends to be more compact and economical. However, centralized BMS has drawbacks. Since all batteries are directly connected to BMS, BMS requires many ports to connect to all battery packs. The result is a large battery pack containing a large number of wires, cables, connectors, etc., making both troubleshooting and maintenance difficult.

**Modular BMS Topology**

BMS is divided into multiple replicated modules, each with its wire bundle, connected to adjacent assigned parts of the battery stack. In some cases, these BMS submodules may reside under a primary BMS module oversight whose function is to monitor the status of the submodules and communicate with peripheral equipment.

**Primary/Subordinate BMS**

Conceptually similar to the modular topology, however, in this case, the slaves are more restricted to just relaying measurement information, and the master is dedicated to computation and control, as well as external communication.

**Distributed BMS Architecture**

A distributed BMS incorporates all the electronic hardware on a control board placed directly on the cell or module that is being monitored. This reduces most wiring to a few sensor wires and communication wires between adjacent BMS modules. As a result, each BMS is more independent and handles calculations and communications as needed. However, despite this apparent simplicity, this integrated form does make troubleshooting and maintenance potentially problematic, as it resides deep inside a shield module assembly. Costs also tend to be higher as there are more BMSs in the overall battery pack structure.

## Advantages of Battery Management Systems

The entire battery energy storage system, often referred to as BESS, consists of dozens, hundreds, or even thousands of strategically coupled lithium-ion cells, depending on the application. These systems may have a voltage rating of less than 100V but could be as high as 800V, with pack supply currents ranging as high as 300A or more. Mishandling high voltage packages can result in life-threatening and catastrophic disasters. Therefore, BMS is absolutely important to ensure safe operation. The advantages of BMS can be summarized as follows.

**Functional safety:** Undoubtedly, functional safety is essential for large format lithium-ion battery packs. However, even small formats such as those used on laptops are known to ignite and cause enormous damage. The personal safety of users of products, including lithium-ion battery systems, leaves little room for battery management errors.

**Durability and reliability:** The electrical and thermal protection management of the battery pack ensures that all cells are used within the declared SOA requirements. This careful monitoring protects the cell from aggressive use and rapid charge and discharge cycles, which inevitably provides a stable system that can provide long-standing reliable service.

**Performance and range:** Optimal battery capacity can be achieved with BMS battery pack capacity management, which uses cell-to-cell balancing to equalize the SOC of adjacent cells across the pack assembly. Without this BMS feature, which accounts for managing self-discharge, charge/discharge cycles, temperature effects, and general aging fluctuations, the battery pack may eventually become unusable.

**Diagnostic, data acquisition, and external communication:** Oversight tasks include continuous monitoring of all battery cells. Data logging can be used by BMS for diagnostics, computation to estimate the SOC of all cells in the assembly. This information is leveraged for balancing algorithms. Collectively this information can be relayed to external devices and displays to indicate the energy available, estimate the expected range or range/ lifetime based on current usage, and provide the state of health of the battery pack.

**Cost and warranty reductions:** The introduction of a BMS into a BESS adds costs. Battery packs are expensive and potentially hazardous. The more complex the system, the higher the security requirements and the more BMS monitoring presence required. But the protection and preventive maintenance of a BMS regarding functional safety, lifespan and reliability, performance and range, diagnostics, etc. guarantee that it will drive down overall costs, including those related to the warranty.

## Battery Recycling

With the spread of Electric Vehicles, the battery recycling market has the potential to grow. Widespread recycling of batteries prevents hazardous materials from entering the waste stream, both at the end of the battery's useful life and during production. Material recovery from recycling will also reintroduce critical materials into the supply chain and increase the domestic source of such materials. Work is underway to develop a battery recycling process that minimizes the life cycle impact of using lithium-ion and other types of batteries in vehicles. However, the recycling processes are not all the same, and material recycling requires different separation processes.

**Smelting:** The smelting process recovers the basic elements or salts. These processes are currently in operation on a large scale and can accommodate multiple types of batteries, including lithium-ion and nickel-metal hydride. Smelting takes place at high temperatures, where organic materials such as electrolytes and carbon anodes burn as fuel or reducing agents. Valuable metals are recovered and sent for purification. Other substances, including lithium, are found in slag and are currently used as additives in concrete.

**Direct Recovery:** These recycling processes directly recover battery-grade materials. Ingredients are separated by various physical and chemical processes and all active materials and metals can be recovered. Direct recovery is a low-temperature process with minimal energy requirements.

**Intermediate process:** The third type of process lies between the two extremes. Such processes may accept multiple kinds of batteries, unlike direct recovery, but recover materials further along the production chain than smelting does.

Separating different types of battery materials is often an obstacle to the recovery of high-value materials. Therefore, for EVs to succeed in terms of sustainability, it is important to design the battery with disassembly and recycling in mind. Standardizing battery, material, and cell design make recycling easier and cheaper.

# XVII

# Controllers for Electric Vehicles

The power generation mechanism of an electric vehicle is very simple as compared to conventional vehicles. It consists of just two components: the motor that provides the power and the controller that controls the power. Whereas the power system of gasoline-powered vehicles consists of several components, such as the engine, carburetor, oil pump, water pump, cooling system, starter, exhaust system, etc. The electric vehicle controller is the power electronic device operating between the batteries and the motor to control the electric vehicle's speed, acceleration, and performance. The controller will also reverse the motor rotation, and convert the motor to a generator (so that the kinetic energy of motion can be used to recharge the battery when the brake is applied). For AC Motor, the controller transforms the direct current into AC along with battery energy flow regulation. For a DC motor, the main function of the controller is to regulate power flow from the battery.

In the early electric vehicles with DC motors, a simple variable-resistor-type controller was there to control the acceleration and speed of the vehicle. With this type of controller, current and power were drawn from the battery. At high speed only, maximum power was getting utilized. At slow speeds, when full power was not needed, high resistance was used to reduce the current to the motor. With this type of controller, a large percentage of the energy from the battery was wasted as an energy loss in the resistor. Modern controllers adjust speed and acceleration by an electronic process called pulse width modulation. Switching devices such as silicone-controlled rectifiers rapidly interrupt (turn on and turn off) the electricity flow to the motor. High power (high speed and/or acceleration) is achieved when the intervals are short. Low power (low speed and/or acceleration) occurs when the intervals are longer.

The Motor Controller's objective is to govern in some predetermined manner, the performance of an electric motor. The main functions of the Motor Controller are:

1. Motor Starting.
2. Motor Stopping.
3. Selecting Forward/Reverse Rotation for Motor.
4. Regulating Speed.
5. Regulating Torque.
6. Regulating Power.
7. Limiting Torque.
8. Protection against overloads.

Motor Controller is a power electronics and embedded micro-computing device which makes the efficient conversion of energy stored in batteries of an electric vehicle to generate motion. Motor, Battery, Throttle, Brake Switch, Forward/ Reverse Switch, etc. are connected to Motor Controller. Apart from energy delivery from the Battery to the Motor, Controller also manages the energy from the motor back to the battery (Energy Recovery) during Regenerative Braking. Motor Controller ensures precise control of Motor Power, RPM, Torque & Direction. And that is why there are various sub-parts in Motor Controller. The main parts of the motor controller are:

Microprocessor Block: Microprocessor block is the heart of the Motor Controller. It has embedded firmware. The main objective of the microprocessor is to realize all the functionalities of the Motor Controller.

Power Electronics Block: This block is made of power electronics devices. In simple words, this block is a bi-directional power converter. The main objective of this block is energy transfer.

Input Interface Block: It helps to connect electronic devices and interfaces to the Motor Controller.

Sensing & Protection Block: This block measures various parameters of the system (e.g. Current/Voltage/Speed). All these parameters are precisely monitored and controlled by Motor Controller. A fault detected will trigger self-protection ensuring vehicle & passenger safety.

Communication Block: This block is the most important part of the Motor Controller. It facilitates the communication of controller data with external systems. Smart controllers are coming with an advanced Communication Block for Autonomous & CASE Mobility.

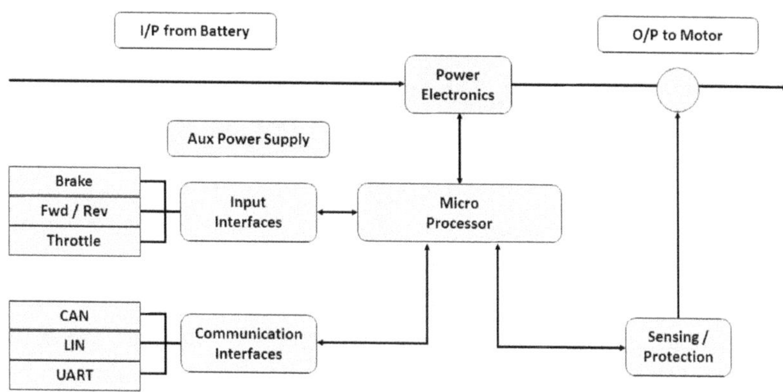


Figure 10 - Motor Controller Architecture

# XVIII
# Converters for Electric Vehicles

Conventional vehicles used around the world continue to cause serious problems for the environment and human life. Air pollution, global warming, and the rapid depletion of global oil resources are serious problems today. Electric vehicles (EVs), hybrid electric vehicles (HEVs), and fuel cell electric vehicles (FCEVs) are usually proposed to replace traditional vehicles shortly. Most electrical and hybrid electrical configurations use two energy storage devices. One is the Main Traction battery and the other one is Auxiliary Battery. The battery is a DC power source. For AC Motors, DC/AC Power conversion is required via a dedicated inverter circuit or integrated inverter circuit along with the controller. In addition, intermediate Sub-Circuits or Auxiliary Battery Charging Circuit need a voltage lesser than the Main Traction Battery Voltage. Thus we need a DC-DC Converter. DC-DC converters can interface the elements in the electric power train by boosting or chopping the voltage levels. For automotive applications, a power converter should be reliable, lightweight, small capacity, highly efficient, have low electromagnetic interference, and have low current/voltage ripple. In electrical engineering, a DC to DC converter is a category of power converters. It is an electric circuit that converts a source of direct current (DC) from one voltage level to another, by storing the input energy temporarily and then releasing that energy to the output at a different voltage. The storage may be in either magnetic field storage components (inductors, transformers) or electric field storage components (capacitors).

Uni-Directional DC-DC Converters are designed to transfer power in only one direction, from the input to the output. A bi-directional converter can move power in either direction. It is useful in applications requiring regenerative braking.

## DC/DC converters for electric vehicles

DC/DC converters can be designed to transfer power from the input to the output. The amount of power flow between the input and output can be controlled by adjusting the duty cycle (ratio of on/off time of the switch). This is typically done to control the output voltage, input current, and output current, or to maintain constant power. Transformer-based converters can separate inputs and outputs. The main drawbacks of converters include complexity, electronic noise, and the high cost of some topologies.

## Types of DC/DC Converters

### *1) Non-Isolated Converters*

Non-isolated converters are commonly used when the voltage needs to be increased or decreased in relatively small ratios (less than 4: 1). There is no dielectric separation between the output and the input. There are five main types of non-isolated converters:

1. Buck (To lower the voltage).
2. Boost (To raise the voltage).
3. Buck-Boost (Either to step down or step up the voltage).
4. Cuk (A type of buck-boost converter with low ripple current).
5. Charge pump (Either to step-up the voltage or inverse, but only in relatively low power applications).

### *2) Isolated Converters*

An isolated converter is used where the output needs to be completely isolated from the input. High-frequency transformers are typically used for this type of converter. There are various types of isolated converters:

1. Half-Bridge (Can supply an output voltage either higher or lower than the input voltage and provide electrical isolation via a transformer).
2. Full-Bridge (One of the commonly used configurations that offer isolation in addition to stepping up or down the input voltage).
3. Fly-back (Uses mutually coupled inductor).
4. Forward (A switching power supply circuit that transfers the energy from the primary to the secondary while the switching element is "on").
5. Push-Pull (One of the oldest switching topologies, and it can give multiple outputs with a single input).

## Design consideration for EV Converters

- Lightweight.
- High efficiency.
- Small volume.
- Low electromagnetic interference.
- Low current ripple drawn from the Fuel Cell or the battery.
- The function of the converter.

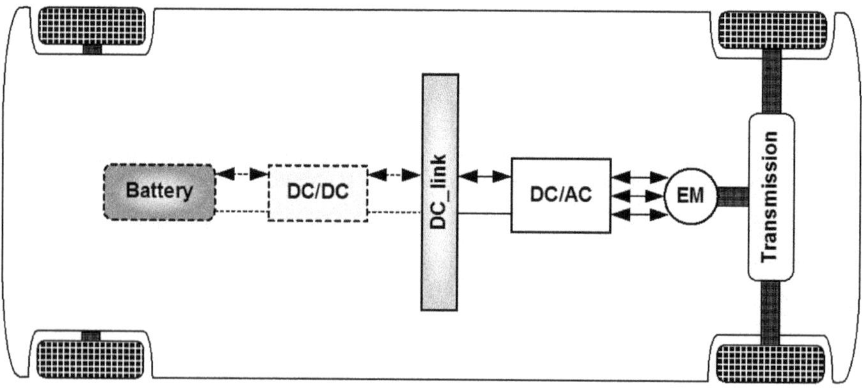


Figure 11 - Converters for EV

# XIX

# Chargers for Electric Vehicles

Batteries store electrical energy in the form of chemical energy and can convert chemical energy back into electrical energy. Converting chemical energy into electrical energy is called discharge. Due to the chemical reaction during discharge, electrons flow to the external load connected to the terminal, and the current flows in the direction opposite to the flow of electrons. Some batteries can return these electrons by passing a reverse current. This process is called charging. The capable batteries to get back electrons in the same electrode are called chargeable and if they are not capable to do this, are called non-rechargeable. In batteries, the electrode where reduction occurs is called the cathode, and the electrode where oxidation occurs is called the anode. Charging Methods for batteries depend on the Chemistry of the Battery.

## Lead Acid Battery

When the battery is connected to a load, the battery begins to discharge. The sulfuric acid (H2SO4) breaks into two parts, hydrogen (2H++) ions and sulfate ions (SO4— ). The hydrogen ion takes an electron from the positive electrode and sulfate ions give an electron to the negative plate. This inequality of electrons causes the flow of current at external load to balance the inequality of electrodes. The Charging begins when the Charger is connected to the positive and negative terminals. The lead-acid battery converts the lead sulfate ($PbSO4$) at the negative electrode to lead (Pb). At the positive terminal, the reaction converts the lead sulfate ($PbSO4$) to lead oxide. The chemical reactions are revers from discharging process.

## *Charging Methods for Lead Acid Battery*

**Constant Voltage:** As the name implies, this method provides a constant voltage till the current taken by the battery goes to zero. It takes a long time.
**Constant Current:** As the name implies, this method supplies a constant current till the voltage reaches its defined gassing voltage. It also takes a long time.

**Multi-level Constant Current:** In this method, the charging current is constant as the voltage reaches the gassing voltage then the current starts to reduce in steps to maintain the voltage. This charger is complicated to build.

**Modified Constant Voltage-Current:** In this method, the battery is charged in three stages. The first stage is the constant current stage. In the second stage, the voltage is constant. Then the voltage will reduce to floating voltage to maintain the battery charged.

## Li-Ion Battery

In Lithium-Ion Battery, the positive electrode (cathode) is made of lithium cobalt oxide and the negative electrode (anode) is made of graphite. Lithium salt as an organic solvent is used as an electrolyte. A separator is used to separate electrodes The nominal voltage of the lithium-ion battery is 3.60V. When the battery is in full charge the voltage is about 4.2 V. when the battery is fully discharged the voltage is about 3.0V. Li-ion battery comes in different sizes, shapes, and the capacity. At the time of discharge of the battery, the Load is connected to the battery terminals. The lithium-ion is released from the negative electrode and travels to the electrolyte. This lithium-ion is absorbed by a positive electrode. The negative electrode also releases the electrons which travel through an external wire to the positive electrode. This provides us with an electric current to the circuit. At the time of charging the Li-ion battery, the battery is connected to the charger. The Positive electrode losses a negatively charged electron. An equal number of positively charged ions are dissolved into the electrolyte solution to maintain this charge balance at the negative electrode side. These lithium-ion travel over to the positive electrode, where they are absorbed within the graphite. This absorption reaction also deposits electrons into the graphite anode to 'tie' up the lithium-ion.

## *Charging Methods for Li-Ion Battery*

The Li-ion battery charging chemistries utilize constant current and constant voltage algorithms that can be divided into four parts:

**Trickle Charge:** When the battery is deeply discharged below 3.0 V per cell, the constant current of 0.1C maximum is used to charge the battery, it is called trickle charge.

**Constant Current:** When voltage is above 3.0V per cell, the constant current is applied in the range of 0.2 C to 1C to perform constant current charging.

**Constant Voltage:** When voltage is reached at 4.2 V per cell from constant current charging. The constant voltage is applied till the current taken by the cell drop to zero, this maximizes the performance of the battery.

**Charge Termination:** The end of charging is detected by an algorithm that detects the current range (that drops from 0.02C to 0.07C) or uses a timer method.

## Electric Vehicle Supply Equipment

Electric Vehicle Supply Equipment Delivers electrical energy from an electricity source to charge EV batteries. It communicates with the EV to ensure that an appropriate and safe flow of electricity is supplied. EVSE units are commonly referred to as "charging stations."Charging is nothing but a Range addition to an EV.

**The charging Methodology depends on**

- The Vehicle.
- The Battery Type.
- Type of EVSE.

## Level 1 EVSE

Level 1 provides alternating current (AC) electricity to the vehicle, with the vehicle's onboard equipment (charger), converting AC to the direct current

(DC) needed to charge the batteries. Level 1 EVSE provides charging through a 120-volt (V) AC plug. Most EVs will come with a Level 1 EVSE cord set so that no additional charging equipment is required. On one end of the cord is a standard, three-prong household plug (NEMA 5-15 connector). On the other end is a J1772 standard connector. Level 1 Charging adds 2 to 5 miles of range per hour of charging. It is the simplest form of charging, using a 120V AC connection to a standard residential/commercial electrical outlet capable of supplying 15-20 amps of current, for a 1.4 kW power when charging.

**Advantages**

- Low installation cost.
- Low impact on electric utility peak demand charges.

**Disadvantages**

- Charging is slow - around 3 or 5 miles of range added per hour of charging.

## Level 2 EVSE

Level 2 EVSE can easily charge a typical EV battery overnight, and it will be a common installation for home, workplace, fleet, and public facilities. Level 2 also provides alternating current (AC) electricity to the vehicle, with the vehicle's onboard equipment (charger) converting AC to the direct current (DC) needed to charge the batteries. Level 2 EVSE offers charging through a 240-V (typical in residential applications) or 208-V (typical in commercial applications) electrical service. These installations are generally hard-wired for safe operation. Level 2 EVSE requires the installation of charging equipment and a dedicated circuit of 20 to 80 amp (A) depending on the EVSE requirements. Level 2 equipment uses the same connector on the vehicle as Level 1 equipment. Level 2 charging adds 10 to 20 miles of range per hour of charging.

**Advantages**

- Charge time is significantly faster than Level 1. EVs will get between 10 and 20 miles of range per hour of charge.
- More energy-efficient than Level 1 for short duration charge events.

**Disadvantages**

- Installation costs are higher than Level 1 and are highly variable depending on equipment and installation issues.
- Potentially higher impact on electric utility peak demand charges.

## DC fast-charging EVSE

DC fast-charging EVSE (480-V AC input to the EVSE) enables rapid charging at sites such as heavy traffic corridors and public fueling stations. A DC fast charger adds 60 to 80 miles of range in 20 minutes of charging. DC fast charging is governed by the North American SAE J1772 Combo standard and the Japanese JEVS G105-1993 standard. DC fast-charge stations generally support both standards. All carmakers adhere to one of these standards, except Tesla, which has developed a higher-performance charging station but offers a CHAdeMO adapter as an option.

**Advantages**

- Charge time is reduced drastically – typically 30 minutes for an 80% charge.

**Disadvantages**

- Equipment and installation costs are higher than level 1 and level 2 charging.
- Increased peak power demand charges from electric utility.
- Competing standards are confusing to EV buyers and charging station operators.
- Potential issues with cold-weather operation requiring increased charging time.

## Inductive Charging

Inductive-charging EVSE uses an electromagnetic field to transfer electricity to an EV without a cord. Wireless EV charging requires an induction coil that creates an alternating EM field from the charging pad.

Meanwhile, a second induction coil in the vehicle receives the EM field from the charging pad, effectively recharging the vehicle batteries after the system converts the EM fields to electric currents. Electrical power from the mains supply is first rectified into a DC voltage to maximize its real power using an AC/DC rectifier and a power factor correction circuit (PFC). This DC signal is then input into a high-frequency inverter to be up-converted to the operating frequency of interest. Compensation networks are then required to help operate the inductive link in resonance conditions. An AC–DC rectifier is utilized after the LCC compensation, in order to convert the coupled AC power to DC power that can charge the EV battery.

**Advantages:**

- No need to carry a bulky charging cable.
- Convenient to use the charger.
- Safe since the absence of a wired connection.
- Maintenance-free.
- Immune to dirt and water.

**Disadvantages:**

- Standardization of charging system.
- The difficulty of installation of a wireless charging system.
- The vehicle has to park in the exact location where charger coils installed to charge the battery.

## Private & Public EV Charging Station

A private station is a station purchased by an individual for personal use. A public station is a shared station; it may be installed on public or private property by a public organization or a company.

## Charging station selection criteria

- The power required (charging time, vehicle capacity, pricing).
- The communication requirements (access control, payment system, help system).

- The number of cables and plugs (for shared-access stations).

## Charging Station Costs

Various costs involved in setting up a charging station are:

- Installation Cost.
- Operation Cost.
- Maintenance Cost.
- Electricity Cost.

## Steps for setting up EVSE

- Choosing an EVSE Provider and Electrical Contractor.
- Performing Energy Audit.
- Performing EVSE and Electrical Upgradations.
- Engineering and Construction.
- Site and Equipment Considerations.
- Complying with Regulations.
- Installation, Operation & Maintenance.

## Charging Station Locations and Hosts

- Governments.
- Office Parks.
- Parking Garages.
- Home Owners' Associations.
- Retail Stores.

## EV Charging Station Benefits

- Customer Attraction and Retention, Corporate Branding.
- User Charging and Parking Fees.
- Employee Attraction and Retention.
- Fleet Cost Savings.
- Advertising Opportunities.
- Contribution to LEED Certification.
- Value of Avoided Carbon Emissions.
- Improved Public Health.
- Increased Energy Security.

## Site and Equipment Considerations

- Ventilation.
- Avoiding Hazards.
- Convenience.
- Accessibility.
- Battery Temperature Limits.
- Pooled Water and Irrigation.
- Preventing Impact.
- Lighting and Shelter.
- Vandalism.
- Trouble Reporting.

# XX

# Design of Powertrain for Electric Vehicle

In electric vehicles, the main components are motors, batteries, controllers, converters, and chargers. When designing an electric vehicle, the first and most important component to choose is the electric vehicle powertrain. This is because the internal combustion engine of a traditional vehicle has been replaced by the powertrain of an electric vehicle. Therefore, the electric powertrain used in electric vehicles must generate the appropriate power and other characteristics needed for traction purposes. An important task is to select the appropriate powertrain rating based on the load you carry.

## EV Powertrain Design Methodology

**1) Motor Selection**

Motor selection is the first step. It consists of the following calculations.

a) Vehicle Weight Calculation
b) Motor Power Calculation
c) Motor Torque Calculation
d) Motor RPM Calculation
e) Motor Voltage Calculation
f) Motor Current Calculation

**2) Battery Selection**

Battery selection is a very crucial step. It consists of the following calculations.

a) Battery Power Calculation
b) Battery Voltage Calculation
c) Battery Capacity Calculation
d) Battery Charging Time Calculation
e) Battery Range Calculation
f) Battery Discharge Time Calculation

**3) Controller Selection**

Controller selection includes the following calculations.

a) Power Rating Calculation
b) Current Rating Calculation
c) Voltage Rating Calculation

**4) Charger Selection**

Charger selection included the following calculations.

a) Charger Power Calculation
b) Charging Supply Calculation
c) Charging Voltage Calculation
d) Charging Current Calculation

**5) Transmission Selection**

Transmission selection includes the following calculations.

a) Gear Ratio Calculation
b) Power Transmission Calculation
c) Power Losses Calculation

## EV Powertrain Development Methodology

1) EV Powertrain Design Mechanical Calculations
2) EV Powertrain Design Electrical Calculation
3) EV Powertrain CAD
4) EV Powertrain Modeling
5) EV Powertrain Simulation
6) EV Powertrain Analysis
7) EV Powertrain Component Selection
6) EV Powertrain Prototype
7) EV Powertrain Development
8) EV Powertrain Integration
8) EV Powertrain Testing & Certification

## EV Powertrain Calculation

The power is made available to the battery through the charging module. The battery supplies electric power to the motor through a motor controller, which helps in controlling the input and output parameters of the motor. The output mechanical power from the motor is given to the wheel through a drive shaft. In this way, electric power flows through various components in an electric vehicle and gets converted into mechanical power. The required power for moving vehicles is subjected to many rules. These rules are interrelated with tires, friction, wind resistance, weight, and inclination level.

**1) Mass Calculation**

The total mass of the Vehicle (Inclusive of Driver, Passenger, Seats, Body, Chassis, Suspension, Brakes, Steering, Battery, Motor, Controller, Converter, Charger & Other Components) that has to be driven by an electric motor of an EV.

**2) Rolling Resistance Calculation**

Fr = m * g * Cr

Pr = Fr * V

Where

m = mass of vehicle (Kg)

g = gravitational Forces (m/s^2)

Cr = coefficient of rolling resistance (Constant)

V= speed in m/s

*Factor Affecting coefficient of Rolling Resistance*

- Weight of vehicle
- Speed of vehicle
- Tyre pressure
- Surface roughness of Road
- Vehicle tire rubber hardness

**3) Air Resistance Calculation**

Fa= 0.5*Cd*Af*ρ*(V)^2

Pa = Fd * V

Where

Cd=coefficient of drag

ρ= density of air

Af= vehicle frontal area

V= speed in m/s

*Factors Affecting the Cd*

- Density of Air
- Frontage Area of Vehicle
- Velocity of vehicle

*Cd value will be different in different conditions.*

**4) Gradient Resistance Calculation**

Fg= m*g*Sin (α)

Pg = Fg* V

Where

m= mass of the vehicle

g= acceleration due to gravity

α= gradient angle in degree

V= speed in m/s

**5) Total Power**

Total Power = Pr + Pa + Pg

**6) Total Torque**

T= (60*P)/(2 *π *N)

**7) Battery Size**

Battery Size (Ah) = (Watt* Hour)/Voltage

Where

Watt= total load on the battery

hour=backup time

Voltage=voltage rating of the battery

**8) Battery Charging Time**

*Charging Time [h] = Battery Capacity [kWh] / Charging Power [kW]*

## EV Powertrain Homologation

Homologation refers to the approval required for a vehicle before sales and marketing. This is done to ensure that the vehicle meets the official standards set by the relevant regulatory body. This standard aims to improve vehicle safety, manage environmental impacts and evaluate the component quality and manufacturing processes. The process of testing and certification for conformance to technical standards is known as type approval. The homologation process for any automotive vehicle including Electric Vehicles consists of various steps.

1. Component approval (e.g. lamps, mirrors, tires).

2. Component fitting to the vehicle (e.g. electric/electronic sub-assemblies, car audio systems).
3. System approvals (e.g. for breaking mechanism).
4. Whole vehicle type approval (WVTA) / Vehicle certification test.

For each step, the concerned authority will issue a system approval according to the respective Centre Motor Vehicle Rules (CMVR). The approvals are based on test reports prepared by an officially recognized testing organization. Once all approvals are collected, the testing organization issues the report for approval as a basis for the homologation certificate.

**Homologation Agencies in India:**

1. Automotive Research Association of India (ARAI) at Pune, Maharashtra.
2. Vehicle Research & Development Establishment (VRDE) at Ahmednagar, Maharashtra.
3. International Centre for Automotive Technology (iCAT) at Manesar, Haryana.
4. Global Automotive Research Centre (GARC) at Oragadam near Chennai, Tamil Nadu.
5. National Automotive Test Tracks (NATRAX) at Pithampur near Indore, Madhya Pradesh.
6. National Institute of Automotive Inspection, Maintenance & Training (NIAIMT) at Silchar, Assam.

# XXI
# EV Safety & Maintenance

Maintenance needs and safety requirements for plug-in hybrid electric vehicles (PHEVs) and hybrid electric vehicles (HEVs) are similar to conventional vehicles, while all-electric vehicles (BEV) require less maintenance. Manufacturers are designing these vehicles and publishing guidelines keeping maintenance and safety in mind. Electric vehicles are a completely different technology than internal combustion engines, which means that there may be new safety risks primarily related to high-power electrical equipment characteristics. Electric vehicle systems should be designed to function safely under all conditions. Currently, the standards and official regulations for electric vehicles are not yet clearly defined. Another important aspect is the psychological awareness of these "new" risks. In urban traffic, due to their environmental benefits, electric vehicles are an important factor for mobility improvement and a healthier living environment. The different risks associated with this technology must be carefully assessed.

**Electric Vehicle Safety Classification:**

- Electric system safety
- Functional system safety
- Battery safety
- Vehicle maintenance & operation safety

## Electric system safety

In Electric Vehicle, depending on the type & architecture of the Electric vehicle, system voltage will vary. For example:

- Electric Bicycle: 24 V - 36 V.
- Electric Motorcycle: 48 V -72 V.
- Electric Three-Wheeler: 48 V -72 V.
- Electric Small Four Wheeler: 48 V - 120 V.
- Electric Large Four Wheeler: 96 V - 240 V.
- Electric Bus: 300 V - 600 V.

In the automotive industry, high-voltage refers to voltages above 60 V DC. At this level contact protection is mandatory. The voltages used on electric vehicles are thus potentially dangerous and measures should be taken to prevent electrocution through direct or indirect contact.

**Protection against direct contact**

Live parts of the electric traction system should be protected against direct contact by persons in or outside the vehicle, through insulation or inaccessible position. Insulation or barriers must be there for protection against direct contact. The conventional protection degrees (IPXXB or IPXXD) should be enforced. Protection degree IPXXD means protection from contact with high voltage live parts provided by either an electrical protection barrier or an enclosure and tested using a Test Wire (IPXXD). Protection degree IPXXB means protection from contact with high voltage live parts provided by either an electrical protection barrier or an enclosure and tested using a Jointed Test Finger (IPXXB). Access to live electrical equipment shall only be possible with tools or keys.

**Protection against indirect contact**

The problem of indirect contacts is mainly related to the problem of frame faults. Any false connection between the traction circuit and the vehicle frame is regarded as a fault. Frame faults can lead to several hazards:

- Short circuits.
- Electrocution.
- Uncontrolled operation.

The following measures should be taken to avoid these hazards:

- A fuse of proper rating shall be built inside the battery pack.
- The vehicle frame shall be isolated from the traction circuit.
- All conductive parts of the vehicle shall be connected with an equipotential connection.
- Frame fault leakage detection shall be included in routine maintenance.
- Permanent frame fault monitoring is mandatory for certain vehicles.

## Functional system safety

The electric vehicle traction system must ensure a reliable and safe operation of the vehicle. The architecture of the tractive system in an electric vehicle is fundamentally different from ICE vehicles and specific measures should be taken to avoid or prevent unsafe operations.

**Tractive System Actuation Safety:**

An electric vehicle won't make a noise like a conventional vehicle at the start or during operation. To prevent movement through unintentional actuation of the traction circuit, a warning device shall be present.

**Power Flow Safety:**

To avoid possible damage through excessive torque, overcurrent, or fierce accelerations, the power flow must be adequately organized. It shall be impossible to activate the controller with the accelerator depressed. Any unintentional movement of the vehicle during start-up shall be avoided.

**Fierce Reverse Braking Safety:**

The change of driving direction in an electric vehicle can be done mechanically or electrically. While driving backward, prevention of fierce reverse braking must be achieved through an electrical safety device that only allows reverse to be engaged when the vehicle speed is lower.

**Emergency & Safety:**

Emergency switches are essential in EVs. An emergency stop switch is a safety mechanism used to shut off EVs in an emergency when they cannot be shut down in the usual manner. The purpose of an emergency push button is to stop the EV quickly when there is a risk of injury or the workflow requires stopping. The disconnect action must be direct and its operation shall not be damaging to the controller.

Emergency switches come in different forms:

- Battery connectors.
- Direct-acting emergency buttons.
- Indirect-acting emergency buttons.

**Power Surge Safety:**

Unintentional acceleration due to failures in electronic traction controllers must be prevented by the use of power surge control fail-safe circuitry.

**Regenerative Braking Safety:**

Safety & efficiency must be ensured during energy recovery in the process of Regenerative Braking.

**Frame Faults Safety:**

Frame faults and stray currents can also cause uncontrolled operation. A fault current of a few μA in a controller can release hundreds of Amps in the motor.

**High Voltage & Low Voltage Circuit Safety:**

Traction and auxiliary circuits shall be galvanically isolated to avoid stray currents.

**Electromagnetic Interference Safety:**

Electromagnetic interference, generated externally or by the controller itself, must not adversely affect controller operation.

**Overspeeding Safety:**

Electric motors, particularly DC motors, can be liable to overspeeding damage.

## Battery safety:

The battery is the most critical item in an electric vehicle. It represents several potential hazards like electrical, mechanical, chemical, and explosion hazards.

**Battery electrical hazard safety:**

- Protection against electric shock: Enclosures shall be enforced as needed in Battery.
- Protection against short-circuits: Protective devices (fuse links) shall be provided.

**Battery mechanical hazard safety:**

The traction battery is a heavy item. Its location and position in the EV must be determined considering the instability of the vehicle, injury in case of an accident, and mechanical damage to the cells/battery.

**Battery chemical hazard safety:**

Batteries consist of largely four main components: cathode, anode, electrolyte, and separator. Precautions should be taken during handling. In case of an accident, care must be taken to avoid fire/hazard.

**Battery charging safety:**

During the battery recharging process, the electric vehicle is connected to the main power source or grid. The necessary safety measures should be taken to avoid electrocution danger. We must use proper fusing, galvanic isolation, insulation monitoring & earthing to ensure safe charging.

**Battery explosion hazard safety:**

The battery is widely used in the field of energy storage presently. However, the combustible gases produced by the batteries during the thermal runaway process may lead to explosions. Thermal runaway begins when the heat generated within a battery exceeds the amount of heat that is dissipated to its surroundings. If the cause of excessive heat creation is not remedied, the condition will worsen. The rise in temperature in a single cell will begin to affect other cells nearby, and the pattern will continue, thus thermal runway will happen.

Causes of the thermal runway:

- Battery surrounding temperature
- Age of the Cell.
- Overcharging.

Prevention of thermal runway:

- Scheduled maintenance.
- Continuous monitoring of battery parameters.

## EV maintenance & operation safety:

The electrical system (battery, motor, and associated electronics) typically requires minimal scheduled maintenance. Because PHEVs and HEVs have internal combustion engines, maintenance requirements are similar to those of conventional vehicles.

Battery electric vehicles typically require less maintenance than conventional vehicles because:

- The battery, motor, and associated electronics require little to no regular maintenance.
- Brake wear is significantly reduced due to regenerative braking.
- There are far fewer moving parts relative to a conventional fuel engine.

The advanced batteries used in these vehicles have a limited number of charging cycles (The number of times the battery can be charged and discharged is called "cycle life"). Some vehicle battery systems use liquid coolant to maintain a safe operating temperature. These systems may require regular inspections. EV batteries are typically designed to last the expected life of the vehicle. Commercially available electric vehicles must meet Vehicle Safety Standards and undergo the same rigorous safety tests. Manufacturers are designing these vehicles with insulated high voltage wires and safety features that disable the electrical system in the event of a collision or short circuit detection. All-electric vehicles (BEVs) tend to have a lower center of gravity than traditional vehicles, which makes them more stable and less prone to roll over.

## Regulatory aspects for EV Safety

Standards and regulations for electric vehicles are still under development. There are no specific standards covering electric vehicle safety globally. Several international standardization committees deal with electric vehicle standards.

**International Standards:**

- International Electrotechnical Commission (IEC).
- International Organization for Standardization (ISO).
- European Committee for Standardization (CEN).
- Occupational Safety and Health Administration (OSHA).
- Institute of Electrical and Electronics Engineers (IEEE).
- Society of Automotive Engineers (SAE).

**Indian Standards**

- Bureau of Indian Standards (BIS).
- Automotive Industry Standards (AIS).

## Personal Protective Equipment for EV Safety

When working on an electric or hybrid vehicle, it is important that the technician/engineer is equipped with reliable protective equipment to ensure safe work. Personal Protective Equipment (PPE) is impelled as a final measure for suitable safety precautions when working on EVs. The purpose of this equipment is to protect individuals who work on or near an installation that presents an electrical hazard. The equipment used should be appropriate for the type of operation and voltage level of the installation. The use of improper PPE for a specific hazard can cause significant danger to the user.

The following are important protective equipment needed for ensuring EV Safety.

**1) Gloves**

These are the first line of defense for contact with energized components. Most EV manufacturers recommend that insulated rubber gloves should be worn when working near all high-voltage components, not just the vehicle batteries. Ordinary latex gloves are not thick enough and do not provide sufficient protection from the shock hazard.

Example: Class 0, 1000 V, Insulated Gloves.

**2) Undergloves**

To be worn underneath electrical safety gloves and leather gloves. Cotton under gloves not only reduces sweating but also gives added comfort and protection to the PPE user in warm and humid conditions.

Example: Cotton Underglove.

**3) Overgloves**

These are worn over insulating gloves to protect against mechanical hazards and electrical arcing.

Example: Leather Overgloves.

**4) Face / Eye Shield**

This part of the equipment is extremely important when working on high voltage as it protects the eyes from any 'flash over' that can occur if an electrical spark is produced.

Example: Safety Goggles.

**5) Dielectric Overboots**

To be worn over existing footwear. The dielectric over the boot provides additional protection by preventing electric shocks.

**6) Insulating Rubber Apron**

Manufactured from 1mm thick orange neoprene with a nylon insert for added strength, this apron is to protect technicians working with live voltages up to 1000V.

It is important to maintain PPE and perform regular examinations before and after use to ensure the equipment continues to provide the degree of protection for which it is designed. This may include checking for defaults and cleaning items. If there are any uncertainties, the items should be replaced.

## High Voltage Tools for EV Safety

EVs may differ from one another in terms of features or price, but they all have one thing in common: an HV electrical system. HV is defined as having greater than 30 volts AC or 60 volts DC. Whenever high voltage is there, special protective gear and equipment are required. Specialized tools that are insulated for high voltage are necessary while working on EV. These specialized tools are typically rated for up to 1,000 volts and are either made out of a non-conductive material, such as plastic, or may be coated to insulate them from electricity. Care must be taken with these tools to ensure that their insulative properties are not compromised.

Example:

- High Voltage Screw Driver.
- High Voltage Ratchet Set.
- High Voltage Hand Wrenches.
- High Voltage Needle Nose Plier.
- High Voltage Plier.

In addition to common hand tools, HV systems also require special tools for the measurement of power/voltage/current in the system or subsystems. These tools are not only designed to be insulated from high voltage but they're also designed to safely have high-voltage and current run through them. Care must be taken with these tools to ensure that their properties are not compromised.

Example:

- High Voltage Industrial Multimeter.
- High Voltage Insulation Multimeter.

## First Aid for EV Accident

- First, ensure you are not in danger. Stop 100 meters away from the accident. Turn on your vehicle's warning lights.
- Call the police and ambulance. Don't assume another driver or passer-by has already done so.
- Evaluate the condition of those involved and respond accordingly.
- For fender-benders, providing emotional support is usually enough.
- For more severe accidents, don't try to move injured persons, if this is possible. An exception to this is a potential fire or explosion risk.
- Use the recovery position.
- Start chest compressions or CPR for unresponsive persons who are not breathing. Chest compressions help pump blood throughout the body to deliver oxygen to the brain.
- If you feel confident, provide CPR by combining chest compressions with rescue breaths in cycles of 30 chest compressions and 2 rescue breaths. Continue compressions/CPR until help arrives.
- Stay calm, and stick to the facts. Tell people involved that the ambulance and police are on their way, but don't try to determine who's at fault.
- Last but not least, share key info with the police and ambulance. Focus first on persons who are critically injured.

## Safety Guidelines for EVs

- Do not expose the vehicle to extreme temperatures for an extended period of time.
- Do not leave the vehicle for more than 14 days if the charge of the Li-ion battery is nil or near zero.
- Do not use the Li Battery for any other purpose.

- Unplug both couplers of your Portable Charging Gun before cleaning.
- Do not use a damaged charging station, domestic plug point, or charging port. Both charging gun couplers must fit tightly into receptacles that are in good condition. Using the charger with a worn or damaged port may cause burns or start a fire.
- Ensure that the charging gun is always stored in a safe place. Do not expose it to rain or wet conditions. Avoid pouring or dripping water or other liquids over it.
- If water penetrates the electrical devices, the risk of electric shock increases. Ensure that all plugs and cables are free of moisture before using the charging gun.
- Never connect the charging gun to the mains with wet or moist hands or when the charging gun is wet.
- During charging the vehicle must not be exposed to rain, lightning, and snow.
- To reduce the risk of electrical shock or equipment damage, be cautious while cleaning the connectors and case.
- Do not attempt to start the motor if the vehicle gets flooded due to water.
- Place a High Voltage Warning Sign on the vehicle.
- Contact the nearest Authorised EV Service Centre.

# XXII

# Future Mobility

Transport or transportation is the movement of people, animals, and goods from one location to another. Modes of transport include air, rail, road, water, cable, pipeline, and space. The field can be divided into infrastructure, vehicles, and operations. Transport is important because it enables trade between people, which is essential for the development of civilizations. A well-coordinated system of transport plays an important role in the sustained growth of a country. Transport has recorded extensive growth over the years both in the spread of the network and in the output of the system. Mobility is changing. Nowadays we can simply download an application, register, and use car-sharing/carpooling schemes in many cities. Mobility is transforming the urban landscape and our everyday routines. The future of the Indian transport industry will be shaped by progressive transformations through key disruptive technologies based on Smart & Intelligent transport systems driven by Industry 4.0, Advance Communications, Data analytics, IoT, and artificial intelligence from Hyperloop to autonomous and remotely piloted vehicles. Connected – Autonomous – Shared & Electric Mobility will play an important role in creating a sustainable future for transport. It will help to achieve essential policy objectives such as tackling climate change, fighting congestion, creating economic growth, contributing to the reinventing the industrialization in the Asian continent, and providing mobility to citizens of all ages and social backgrounds. Transport is the backbone of the economy, and the CASE should be the backbone of transport. The next immediate & important step for our country is to create value within the transportation sector, for which improving assets and productivity, reducing costs, and cutting waste are critical. This is where technology can help, enabling effective route and capacity planning, seamless linkages with allied sub-sectors, improving safety and customer experience, reducing pilferage, environmental performance, etc. Driverless, connected cars are leading the way in a new era of travel that is efficient, affordable, clean, and green. Experts predict e-mobility will transform travel in the years to come and shape the future of mobility, smart cities, and interactive communities.

## The Mobility of tomorrow

The Mobility of tomorrow will be fundamentally different from what it is today. We see four major trends hanging in the automotive industry: Connectivity (C), Autonomous driving (A), Shared & Services (S), and Electric Mobility (E). They are summarized under the acronym CASE. Automotive Industry is going through a transformation in order to take a new shape. Companies & Governments are investing in future-oriented CASE fields. All four letters revolve around one theme: how can we ease the lives of our customers and make products and mobility services as comfortable, as efficient, and as intuitive as possible. CASE is not only limited to cars but also for pursued vans, trucks, buses, and financial services. We are convinced that electrification is the future. Thus we are electrifying our cars, trucks, vans, and buses. Every nation is now aiming for emission-free mobility. While working for Pollution Free Nation with EV Transition, there are different approaches leading to the same goal. Optimizing the efficiency of combustion engines, by rolling new engine generation is one way for it. The electrification of the combustion engines with EQ Boost is based on the additional onboard network with a starter/alternator. Hybridization with EQ Power and EQ Power Plus with the latest lithium-ion technology and intelligent battery operating system is a productive way to control emissions. The third way can be the emission-free powertrains with battery electric vehicles and fuel cell vehicles.

## Connected and Autonomous Vehicles

Connected and autonomous vehicles are likely to become a common feature on roads within the next decade, along with the increased use of electric and shared vehicles. Collectively, Connected – Autonomous – Shared & Electric Mobility will have a major impact on the transport network. CASE Mobility will introduce an era of unprecedented change. Therefore, it is vital for Nations to consider how to manage and take advantage of this new technology. CASE will present many opportunities, from making our roads safer to reducing emission levels, as well as the added implications of increasing job creation.

## Advantages of Connected Autonomous Shared Electric Mobility

### *a) Product Evolution*

**Connected Vehicles and Electric Vehicles** are deeply connected. If EV Ecosystem has to be created, then connectivity is the basic ingredient for it. Connectivity helps in Understanding the Product Development, Operation efficiency of the Product, and creating structures for the EV Ecosystem. Taking an example of the very basic form of Connectivity-Telematics: With Matrix coming out of Telematics Data, we are able to understand the behavior of motor, controller, and battery. Using demographics, we can limit various parameters of current-voltage depending on temperature, acceleration, and retardation. Thus product development can be iterated and optimized.

**The application-based product development** approach is feasible with telematics & connected vehicle. If the vehicle is to be used for Food Delivery, Payload, Delivery timing, Environmental Condition, Ride Frequency, and other assessments can help in product development.

**Mode Selection** (City Mode, Town mode, Highway Mode, Hill Mode, etc.) option can also be given depending on secondary data collection, analysis & calculation.

### *b) Operation Efficiency*

Operational efficiency is the key point of EV. EVs will get adopted only when there is a business case around them. Range Anxiety and Cost versus Utilization are the two-point of concern with regard to EVs.

Range Enhancement is very important if we want to have EVs as all-purpose Vehicles in the coming time. Range depends on various parameters of the power train. Motor Performance, Battery Capacity, Voltage Current

Fluctuations, Controller Configuration, etc. How is the vehicle driven is one of the major points in considering vehicle performance in terms of Range? How a driver is using an EV, impacts 20% of its range. The range has two units. One is the range inherently built in the vehicle through a power train, second is the range that gets deployed on road because of driving behavior. Driving Behavior is one of the major parameters impacting range. A fleet operator having an electric asset would be expecting operational efficiency. And operational efficiency can be improved by analyzing perfect driving behavior specifically for an EV. Using Connectivity and Telematics we can access speed, acceleration, deceleration, frequency of stops, dynamic conditions, gradient torque and speed, current, and Voltage. These parameters will be helping in framing driving behavior. And perfect driving behavior will enhance the best possible range.

EVs are at least 1.5 plus times more expensive than ICE Vehicles. We look at expensive assets by utilizing them more. EV utilization can be increased with proper driving, charging and operation. Utilizing it properly will help in extracting potential benefits.

## Structures of EV Ecosystem

When we are focusing on the adoption of EVs, we must be well prepared for the execution. In India with great support from the Government end, companies are building new EVs to roll out on roads. But we must be prepared with the prime factors required for smooth functionality. EV cannot sustain alone without the presence of a complete EV Ecosystem. We need Vehicle Charging Infrastructure, Vehicle Maintenance, Service & Troubleshooting Centers, a Skilled Workforce, an Effective EV Product Market, Effective Economic Models & Services regards to EV, Infrastructure for R&D, etc.

### *a) Charging Infrastructure*

On the basis of the application of an EV, driving behavior, and telematics data analysis, charging infrastructures can be made.

### *b) Remote Diagnosis & Trouble Shooting Centers*

With Connected, Automated, Shared, Electric Vehicles it is very convenient & easy to diagnose as continuous parametric monitoring takes place. Also, the establishment of Trouble Shooting centers with respect to performance matrix, ride length, and charging graphs will be an easy task with connected vehicles.

### *c) Insurance Facility*

Based on data reports of EV components, performance matrix, and dynamic elements, connected vehicles will be aiding insurance companies in confidently ensuring EVs.

### *d) Finance Facility*

The biggest challenge for EVs is getting finance because nobody knows the performance statistics & residual/resell value of an EV. Companies are hunting to fetch data on battery & motor performance after intermittent Cycles. This data is very necessary for fixing risk variables & depreciation schedules. Range versus Battery Cycles, Payload versus Range, Motor Efficiency Curve, and Battery Efficiency Curve- these data can be fetched only through a connected vehicle system.

### *e) Second Life for an EV*

Based on fetched data with respect to EV Performance & Operating Conditions, Second Life for the components or an EV can be provided with resale or reuse.

Indian geography represents a multipurpose transport network. Highways, railways, airways, and waterways feature as the principal transportation systems in India to transport goods and people in, around, and across the country. Transportation in progressing countries is of great gravity because of its contribution to national and regional economic, industrial, social, and cultural development. Deficient transportation facilities detain the process of socio-economic development in a country. Especially in a heavily populated country such as India, managing different aspects of transportation is a difficult task. The mobility of tomorrow needs advanced creative design, shared intelligence, systems engineering, and multi-domain collaboration. Connected Autonomous Shared Electric vehicles will be disrupted in the future mobility ecosystem.

# Bibliography

1) India Transportation, September 23, 2011, The World Bank News. (https://www.worldbank.org/en/news/feature/2011/09/23/india-transportation)

2) History and Evolution of Automobiles, NCERT Book (https://ncert.nic.in/vocational/pdf/ivas101.pdf)

3) Infrastructure, Fiscal Policy & Government Spending, Article By The Investopedia Team, Updated January 07, 2022. (https://www.investopedia.com/terms/i/infrastructure.asp)

4) E-Mobility Programme Article posted by Bureau of Energy Efficiency, Government of India, Ministry of Power. (https://www.beeindia.gov.in/content/e-mobility)

5) The History of the Electric Car, dated September 15, 2014, published by the Department of Energy (https://www.energy.gov/articles/history-electric-car)

6) History of Electric Vehicles (EVs) in India, Article dated September 4, 2021, Written by Sudarshan published by Electric World of Dark (https://electricworldofdark.in/history-of-electric-vehicles-evs-in-india/)

7) Mahindra seeks subsidy to promote electric cars, an article by Business Standard. (https://www.business-standard.com/article/companies/mahindra-seeks-subsidy-to-promote-electric-cars-113112700625_1.html)

8) "How Do Gasoline Cars Work?" 2021. U.S. Department of Energy Alternative Fuels Data Center. Accessed July 6, 2022. (https://afdc.energy.gov/vehicles/how-do-gasoline-cars-work)

9) "How Do Hybrid Electric Cars Work?" 2021. U.S. Department of Energy Alternative Fuels Data Center. Accessed July 6, 2022. (https://afdc.energy.gov/vehicles/how-do-hybrid-electric-cars-work)

10) "How Do Plug-In Hybrid Electric Cars Work?" 2021. U.S. Department of Energy Alternative Fuels Data Center. Accessed July 6, 2022.((https://afdc.energy.gov/vehicles/how-do-plug-in-hybrid-electric-cars-work)

11) "How Do All-Electric Cars Work?" 2021. U.S. Department of Energy Alternative Fuels Data Center. Accessed July 6, 2022. (https://afdc.energy.gov/vehicles/how-do-all-electric-cars-work)

12) "How Do Fuel Cell Electric Vehicles Work Using Hydrogen?" 2021. U.S. Department of Energy Alternative Fuels Data Center. Accessed July 6, 2022. (https://afdc.energy.gov/vehicles/how-do-fuel-cell-electric-cars-work)

13) Types of Motors used in Electric Vehicles, Published May 3, 2019, by Sri Hari Karthik, Circuit Digest. (https://circuitdigest.com/article/different-types-of-motors-used-in-electric-vehicles-ev)

14) What is a Battery Management System?, published by Synopsys. (https://www.synopsys.com/glossary/what-is-a-battery-management-system.html)

15) What is EV BMS and how does it work, published by Maxworld Technologies. (https://www.maxworldpower.com/what-is-ev-bms-and-how-does-it-work/)

16) How rechargeable batteries, charging and discharging cycles work, By Ayush Jain, Engineers Garage. (https://www.engineersgarage.com/how-rechargeable-batteries-charging-and-discharging-cycles-work/)

17) Components of EV Charging Station – Power Electronics, Charge Controller, Network Controller, Cables, Dec 22, 2018, posted by Energy Alternatives Indi (https://www.eai.in/blog/2018/12/components-of-ev-charging-infrastructure.html)

18) DC/DC Converters for Electric Vehicles, Authors: Monzer Al Sakka, Joeri Van Mierlo, and Hamid Gualous. (https://cdn.intechopen.com/pdfs/19583/InTech-Dc_dc_converters_for_electric_vehicles.pdf)

19) EVSE-Detailed-Overview by cleanfuelsohio.org (https://cleanfuelsohio.org/wp-content/uploads/2021/07/EVSE-Detailed-Overview.pdf)

20) First aid basics: What to do in case of an accident posted on 27.06.2016 by ALPHABET. (https://www.alphabet.com/en-ww/blog/first-aid-basics-what-do-case-accident)

21) Global EV & PHEV Sales Data, published by EV-volumes.com (https://www.ev-volumes.com/)

22) Electric Vehicle Sales Figures in India, published by SMEV. (https://www.smev.in/fy-15-21)

# Coefficients

***Cr Standard Values***

Cr = 0.01 up to 500 kg weight

Cr = 0.02 up to 500-1500 kg weight

Cr = 0.03 up to 1500 kg weight

***Cr value in various conditions***

Cr= 0.001 - 0.002 (railroad steel wheels on steel rails)

Cr= 0.001 (bicycle tire on wooden track)

Cr= 0.002 - 0.005 (low resistance tubeless tires)

Cr= 0.002 (bicycle tire on concrete)

Cr= 0.004 (bicycle tire on asphalt road)

Cr= 0.005 (dirty tram rails)

Cr= 0.006 - 0.01 (truck tire on asphalt)

Cr= 0.008 (bicycle tire on rough paved road)

Cr= 0.01 - 0.015 (ordinary car tires on concrete, new asphalt, cobbles small new)

Cr= 0.02 (car tires on tar or asphalt)

Cr= 0.02 (car tires on gravel - rolled new)

Cr= 0.03 (car tires on cobbles - large worn)

Cr= 0.04 - 0.08 (car tire on solid sand, gravel loose worn, soil medium-hard)

Cr= 0.2 - 0.4 (car tire on loose sand)

***Cd value in various conditions***

For Modern car like a Tesla model 3 or model Y, Cd= 0.23

For Toyota Prius, Tesla model S, Cd= 0.24

For Sports car, sloping rear, Cd= 0.2 - 0.3

For Common car like Opel Vectra, Cd= 0.29

For Bus, Cd= 0.6 - 0.8

For Old Car like a T-ford, Cd= 0.7 - 0.9

For Bicycle, Cd= 0.9

For Tractor Trailed Truck, Cd= 0.96

# INFOGRAPHIC

Scan to refer to infographic for all the chapters.

www.ingramcontent.com/pod-product-compliance
Ingram Content Group UK Ltd.
Pitfield, Milton Keynes, MK11 3LW, UK
UKHW022017190726
13853UKWH00005B/1978